The Indian Texans

TEXANS ALL

A Series from the
Institute of Texan Cultures
Sara R. Massey, General Editor

The Indian Texans

James M. Smallwood

TEXAS A&M UNIVERSITY PRESS ❋ COLLEGE STATION

The Ellwood Foundation, Houston, Texas, provided funding
support for the research and writing of this book.

The paper used in this book
meets the minimum requirements
of the American National Standard for Permanence
of Paper for Printed Library Materials, z39.48-1984.
Binding materials have been chosen for durability.

Illustrations on title page and chapter heads are details
from maps by Jack Jackson found on pages 2 and 5.

LIBRARY OF CONGRESS CATALOGING-IN-PUBLICATION DATA

Smallwood, James.
    The Indian Texans / James M. Smallwood.—1st ed.
        p. cm.—(Texans all)
    Includes bibliographical references and index.
    ISBN 1-58544-353-0 (alk. paper)—
    ISBN 1-58544-354-9 (pbk. : alk. paper)
        1. Indians of North America—Texas.   I. University of Texas Institute
of Texan cultures at San Antonio.   II. Title. III. Series.
    E78.T4S6   2004
    976.4004'97—dc22   2003016360

Contents

Illustrations

Foreword

The Institute of Texan Cultures opened in 1968 with exhibits depicting the various cultural groups that settled Texas. The exhibit displays were the result of a massive research effort by many young scholars into the history and culture of Texas. This research served as the basis for what became known as "the ethnic pamphlet series." The series included pamphlets devoted to the Swiss Texans, the German Texans, the Native Texans, the Mexican Texans, the Greek Texans, the Spanish Texans, the African American Texans, the Chinese Texans, and many more. Some years later, several books representing additional cultural groups were produced. These included the Japanese Texans, the Irish Texans, the Polish Texans, and others.

Thirty years later, as staff reviewed the early pamphlets, it became obvious that although the material remained accurate, much more is now known about the people and the contributions of the various cultural groups to Texas, and it was time to do a major revision with a fresh look. Thus emerged the Texans All book set. Organized by world regions, each volume briefly summarizes aspects of the social and cultural contributions made by major groups immigrating to Texas. The book series includes the five distinctive cultural groups that were in Texas or came to Texas before statehood and into the twentieth century: *The Indian Texans, The Mexican Texans, The European Texans, The African American Texans,* and *The Asian Texans.*

The author of each book used an organizational pattern dictated by the content. (*The Indian Texans* is organized chronologically by tribe, for instance.) The content of the books does not follow a traditional history of battles and events in Texas, but rather addresses the cultures and the people as they formed early communities in Texas. The authors incorporated primary sources into the text, and sidebars provide brief biographical or topical sketches. The maps were commissioned as the manuscripts neared completion to illustrate the settlement patterns of the cultural groups in Texas.

Many of the people portrayed in words and photographs are unknown, for these stories are about ordinary people who struggled to build a home and make a living in Texas. The majority of the more than three hundred photographs in the set are from the Institute of Texan Cultures Research Library's extensive collection of over three million images relating to the people of Texas.

The Indian Texans begins in the very early artifacts found in Texas. The artifacts tell the story of the many people who came to the land of Texas before all others. From the creation stories shared by various tribal cultures to the urban Indians, we learn of spirits, kinship, rituals, and ways of living in the natural environment. It is also a harrowing tale of people living in family groups and bands scattered across the land who welcomed strangers into their midst and in return received dogma, disease, and death from their guests. Over eons the first people adapted to survive while continuing traditions passed on by their ancestors, the ancient ones. Transcending our similarities, culture does make people different from each other; Texas is surely big enough for all.

The drums go on.

Sara R. Massey

Preface

I, like many urban Indians, have had interesting experiences being a "Native American." As a mixed-blood born in 1944, I had a complicated heritage. My grandmother was a full-blood Cherokee, and my grandfather was a mixed-blood Cherokee. Over time, some Cherokee chiefs had the name "Smallwood." Of course, Cherokee is an English word. We called ourselves Tsalagi, meaning "principal people" or "first people." My family tree also contained Choctaw blood.

My grandparents lived in a rural area northeast of Dallas. As a child, I visited them during the school year, and as an additional treat I spent several weeks with them every summer. Going to my grandparents' home felt like camping out. Their house had neither electricity nor natural gas. They had no radio, and television remained in the distant future. They did not have any modern kitchen appliances. Granny washed dishes in a dishpan with water boiled on a woodstove. At night, two kerosene lamps provided a little light. In the winter, two wood-burning stoves kept the house warm. I had very little to do at night, so I usually went to bed shortly after sundown.

The summer nights got hot but with my bedroom windows open I tolerated it. Their home had no running water, so my first job in the morning was to go to the well to haul water, sometimes making many trips. With no bathroom in the house, we used a wooden outhouse, a one-holer. At times, pages of a store catalog replaced bath tissue.

Every morning my grandfather roused me from bed at first light. Then I made the trips to the well so Granny could make coffee. Breakfast seemed a feast considering my grandparents' financial circumstances. It usually consisted of eggs, sausage or bacon, biscuits and gravy, fried potatoes, grits, and some kind of homemade jam. My grandfather needed a lot of food. He stood six-foot five-inches tall and weighed about 275 pounds.

After breakfast, I went off to the woods to swim in the stream, to fish, or to hunt. I studied the animals and Mother Earth. I grew up loving the forest. Not much was mine, but the forest was definitely mine. Whatever I took from Mother Nature's forest—fish, fowl, rabbits, squirrels, or other small wild game—usually became our lunch, except we called it dinner. In the woods, I usually found polk or other eatable plants along with nuts, berries, and roots that also went on the dinner table. After dinner, Grandfather lit his pipe and told me stories about the old ways of our tribe. He told the story of my family. Then, off to the woods I went again for more adventure. Almost always, as I roamed around, I found or learned something new. Some encounters were bad, like the times I ran into skunks or porcupines. Most of my encounters were good though, such as getting so close to deer that I could almost pet them. Back to the house by late afternoon, I talked nonstop to both Granny and Grandfather about my day.

At dinner, which we called supper, we had another feast. Granny usually cooked two main dishes like fried chicken, ham, venison, beef roast, or turkey along with side dishes including potatoes with gravy, beans, beets, corn, and cornbread with homemade butter, along with anything else I found in my afternoon explorations. Fried pies made an excellent dessert. I suppose that we did not eat "Indian"; we ate "Southern" instead. Then after listening to a few more stories, and making a couple of trips to the outhouse, bedtime arrived.

Grandfather taught me to catch fish by hand. He taught me to hunt armed only with a knife, a big one. He taught me to be a gatherer of wild foods. He taught me which berries and roots could be eaten and which could not. He showed me how to live in the forest overnight. I spent many nights under the trees by myself. At first I was afraid in the dark, so I slept in a tree. Later, as I learned more, I slept under a tree rather than in it. Grandfather really taught me self-reliance. He taught me that I could survive anything. I could, because I knew the forest.

My father was the oldest of eleven children, with one child dying in infancy. As time passed, I became aware that I probably had more first cousins than practically anyone else in Texas. Often, the entire clan met at my grandparents' house for feasts. So many folks came that not all could eat at the same time. We ate in three shifts with the grown men first. Then the children ate, and the women last. That is just the way it was.

For many years we also had two annual reunions. One occurred about Christmas time, the other in the summer. So many people came that our reunions had to be moved from my grandparents' small house to the basement of a civic building in Garland, Texas, some distance away from the farm.

I was not the oldest boy of my generation in the family. But I became the first to be called a man and to get to eat with the men. One day at a family gathering, my grandfather made a great announcement. He said that I could eat with the men. I was only eleven years old.

I had become a good hunter, a good fisherman, and an excellent gatherer because I knew the forest. Grandfather walked with me into the kitchen. He told me to sit at the right hand of my father just as my father sat at my grandfather's right hand. The older boys, my cousins, envied me. They still ate with the children while I had become a man.

Later, Grandfather talked to me alone. He told me that all the men in the family had accepted me. He said that I had been recognized as a man. He defined the word "man" in great detail. As he did, I finally realized that when he used the term "man," he spoke about my own father. Then came the demand: I now had to act like a man. Even today, sometimes I take an action just because of how my grandfather defined the word "man." Sometimes, I do not take an action for the same reason.

There was no doubt that ours was an Indian family—except for one thing. As a group, we never discussed it. We never discussed our

Native American heritage. We never associated with other Indians. When the children of our family became five or six years old, they learned why. In East Texas at the time, many white people were racists. They seemed to hate blacks. They also seemed to hate Indians. Whites did not segregate Native Americans the way that they segregated blacks, but the hostility and separation were always there.

I remember a little bit about going to kindergarten when I got to be five. My parents taught me my first survival lesson: I was never ever to admit to being any part Indian. They told me if anyone asked about the name "Smallwood," I could say that "Smallwood" was an English name. From that day forward, as I grew up, I never admitted to anyone that a lot of me was Cherokee. After all, as my mother told me, "I did not look Indian."

Then I went to college. As a freshman, I committed my act of defiance against society. On an application form, I had to identify my race. Instead of checking the box marked "white," I checked the "other" box. Then, I wrote "Cherokee Indian, Tsalagi." But, of course, it was too late. I had never lived as an "Indian." Other than knowing my grandfather's stories, I had no place in Native American culture. However, I did eventually piece together a bit of my family history.

My immediate family's closest ancestors once lived in the New York area. The Cherokees there lived as part of the Iroquois Confederation. My people eventually migrated south until they arrived in western North Carolina. They lived there for a time, and then moved across the Appalachian Mountains into Northern Georgia. Many Cherokees remained in North Carolina. To distinguish between those who moved from those who did not, the terms used were the "under-the-hill Cherokees" and the "over-the-hill Cherokees." In time, the two groups grew apart.

In the Indian removals of the 1830s, the federal government forced all eastern tribes like the Cherokees to move west. The removal was called the "Trail of Tears" because so many Indian people died. But my family did not travel the "Trail of Tears." They ran away. They retreated into the mountains of East Tennessee and went deep into the forest. There, they hid while working a tiny patch of land and growing enough food to stay alive. The men hunted and fished to provide more food, and the women gathered food from Mother Earth.

My people went back to Northern Georgia in 1845 when it was safe to return, but everything had changed. Before the removal, my people farmed on tribal land. They owned almost all of what they produced. The family also had a few cows, pigs, and chickens. Now, whites had all the land. My people could do nothing but become sharecroppers or farm laborers on the land owned by others.

Several generations of my family lived in poverty. My people stayed in Georgia until the Great Depression, 1929–40. In 1931, cotton prices dropped to a nickel a pound. My grandfather loaded the family in his old truck and headed west to East Texas. Helped by his children, Grandfather worked another sharecrop farm near Terrell, Texas, a small town about thirty miles east of Dallas.

Thus, my immediate ancestors were not "Treaty Indians." They did not willingly move west to escape the whites. They were not "Trail of Tears" Indians who were forced at gunpoint to move west. My family belonged to the most defiant group of all. They ran away and refused to be "conquered." They cooperated with the government not at all.

As late as the 1950s, my grandmother received a government military pension because one of her brothers had been killed in World War I. She always tore the checks up and mailed them back. She wanted nothing to do with white government. Somewhere along the way my family became isolated. We lost practically all our Indian heritage except for the stories my grandfather told me.

Me? I am a mixed-blood Tsalagi, an identity I buried until college. Today, little remains of my heritage—except that I still do well in the forest.

The Indian Texans

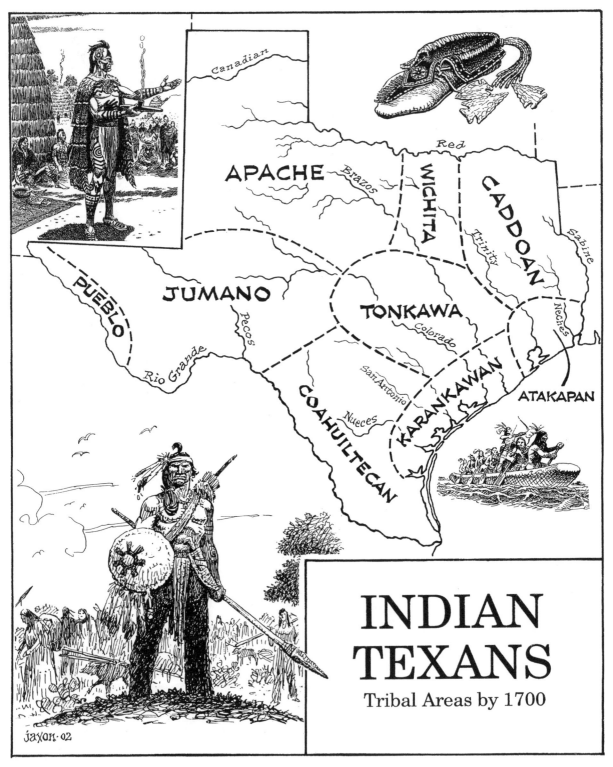

INDIAN TEXANS
Tribal Areas by 1700

Tribal areas before European contact. Map by Jack Jackson

CHAPTER 1

From Prehistory to
Foreign Invasions

*T*HE INDIANS OF TEXAS have a long, rich history that began at least 37,000 years ago, perhaps even earlier. Over the centuries, at least forty different tribes have resided within the borders of Texas. Each had its own unique culture. Some lived as great farmers like the Caddos of East Texas. Others, like the Comanches, traveled great distances and chased the buffaloes across the Great Plains. The Tiguas of the El Paso area lived as village dwellers like their Pueblo ancestors in New Mexico and Arizona. There were the early coastal tribal groups of the Coahuiltecans and Karankawas, who had similar cultures that were distinct from all others. Similarities and differences existed from tribe to tribe, but all played a part in the story of Texas.

As distinct cultural groups, some tribes did not survive into the twentieth century. Some groups warred against others with Indians killing Indians. The first Europeans entered Texas in the 1530s and brought new diseases. The native peoples had no immunity or natural defenses to these foreign diseases. Indians died by the thousands from smallpox, cholera, measles, and other killer diseases.

As pioneers from the United States moved into the area that became Texas, they claimed more and more Indian land. The settlers and the government's Indian policy almost destroyed the many vibrant native cultures. They forced several tribes to leave Texas and move into the Indian Territory, today's Oklahoma, while others moved to Mexico.

Yet the native people remain today. They have worked hard to survive the hardships. For centuries, they endured disgrace, humiliation, and injustices just to preserve their way of life and cultural identity. They struggled to pass their cultural heritage to future generations.

In the early twenty-first century, "survival" has been transformed into "revival." Alone in cities or in the tribal setting, Indians modernize while maintaining the heritage handed down by their forefathers. Even those who were alienated from their tribes are asserting their rights to be Indians. Many now proudly exalt their noble heritage.

THE PALEOINDIAN ERA

Who were the first known people in Texas? This is a difficult question because to find the answer, one must go back to prehistory—events that occurred before written records. Prehistory can only be learned from artifacts such as bones, shards, stones, and other nonperishable objects. Scholars who study the material remains of earlier people are called archaeologists. Archaeologists found fragments of a skull and some bones near Midland, Texas, in 1953, on the Scharbauer Ranch. Archaeologists named the bones "Midland Minnie." She became the first mother of Texas.

Experts disagreed about the time that Minnie lived. Some say she lived between 8,000 to 18,000 years ago. Others say that she lived much earlier. Her skull and bones could be 37,000 years old or even older. The uncertainty of the date got confused even more when construction workers building a dam in North Texas, near Lewisville in Denton County, discovered fourteen rock hearths or fireplaces. When scientists examined the hearths, they found animal bones nearby. Scientists did radioactive carbon tests on the charred wood from the ancient campfires. The tests indicated that the people built the campfires at least 37,000 years ago or maybe even earlier, as the carbon tests were accurate for only 37,000 years! The dating suggested that Minnie had to be at least that old, as carbon tests on artifacts found near her also dated back at least 37,000 years.

▼▼▼

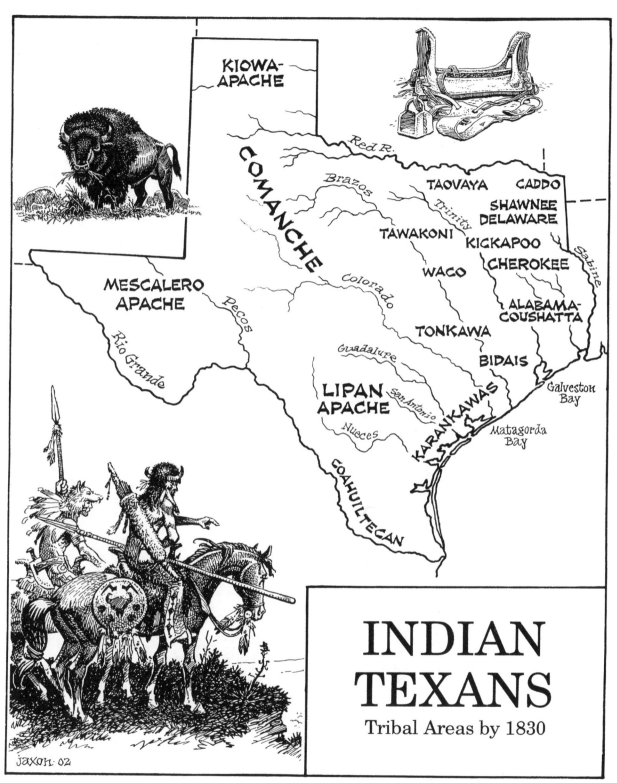

KIOWA-
APACHE

COMANCHE

Red R.

TAOVAYA   CADDO

SHAWNEE
DELAWARE

Brazos

Trinity

TAWAKONI   KICKAPOO

MESCALERO
APACHE

WACO   CHEROKEE

Pecos

Colorado   ALABAMA-
COUSHATTA

Sabine

Rio Grande

TONKAWA

Guadalupe   BIDAIS

LIPAN
APACHE   San Antonio   Galveston
Bay

Nueces   KARANKAWAS   Matagorda
Bay

COAHUILTECAN

JAXON 02

INDIAN
TEXANS
Tribal Areas by 1830

Tribal areas after European contact. Map by Jack Jackson

Burial Sites

▼▼▼

Early groups of people made pictographs or sketches on cave walls showing religious themes. They also left burial sites. Even the early Paleoindians buried their dead. The burial sites found contained not just skeletons but also artifacts, material remains such as tools made from animal bones or other objects. The people believed artifacts buried with the body could be used by the dead person in the afterlife. The artifacts tell us Paleoindians believed in an afterlife. Men and women looked to a god or gods to help them through this world, to help them with problems, and to keep them safe.

Hearths found in Central Texas during a WPA excavation. Institute of Texan Cultures illustration no. 68-36

Plaster cast copy of original skull of "Midland Minnie." Institute of Texan Cultures illustration no. 68-336

If Minnie was the first known mother of Texas, where did she and her people originate? Experts believe that human life originated on the African continent as many as one million years ago. Others say that the human race is at least two million years old. Either way, from Africa, the people fanned out over the world for thousands of years. The early people eventually reached the Middle East, Europe, and Asia. From Asia, they made their way north and crossed into the Western Hemisphere.

Many experts believe the early people of the Americas crossed from Siberia to Alaska by a land bridge, which is covered by the Bering Sea today. President Thomas Jefferson first proposed the "Bering Route Theory." Over eons of time, glaciers extended as far south as today's Iowa. The huge glaciers of frozen water lowered the sea level. When the water lowered there was a 1,300-mile-wide land bridge. The early nomadic peoples trailed the animals that looked for lush vegetation and warm weather. Following the herds, the early people simply walked into the Western Hemisphere.

For thousands of years, the ancient peoples probably wandered back and forth across the land bridge with some staying in today's Alaska while others moved further south and east. They roamed into present Canada and then into the area that became the United States. Eventually, they ended up in Mexico, Central America, and South America. Using only their long spears, they hunted big game like mammoths, elephants, giant bison, and other game that traveled in herds. Experts believe that the early hunters and gatherers completed the entire migration about 10,000 years ago or by 8,000 B.C.

By the historic era, so many different groups of people had come into the New World that at least two hundred "nations" lived here. Each had its own special history, government, language, religion, and traditions.

Anthropologists, who study the history of human culture, call Minnie's people "Paleoindians." *Paleo* means old or first. Coming from Asia, the early people resembled today's Asians.

The earliest people on the continent moved from place to place as nomads. Scholars called them "hunters and gatherers" because the people hunted animals for meat and gathered food from nature. The men hunted huge woolly mammoths, mastodons, and other now-extinct animals. The men also hunted small horses and small camels that also became extinct. Scholars have discovered Paleoindian killing and butchering sites on the high plains of West Texas. The sites add to our knowledge about the very early Indians.

The Paleoindians did almost everything as a group with different jobs for men and women. The men and boys did all the hunting. They also were the fishermen and fished in waters so full of fish they could be caught by hand. The men and boys defended their families from other aggressive humans and fierce animals.

The women and girls gathered food. They studied Mother Earth and collected eatable plants, fruit, berries, nuts, wild onions, wild rice, roots, sunflower seeds, wild tomatoes, and other natural foods. The women and girls cooked the food and made body coverings of animal skins for warmth. The women also cared for their children.

With animals as the major food source the hunt became a very important activity. Near Langtry, Texas, at Eagle's Nest Canyon, archaeologists found a 10,000-year-old bison "jump." The people used the jump as the most effective way of hunting large, dangerous

Drawing of a buffalo jump. Institute of Texan Cultures illustration no. 68-34

animals. Hunters on foot simply stampeded a herd over a cliff. Then the hunters went down into the canyon where they skinned and butchered the animals. Driving animals over a cliff provided the people with large amounts of meat and many hides. The Eagle's Nest bison "jump" is the oldest one of its kind in the United States. Bison then were about three times larger than today's buffalo.

Minnie's people did more than just eat the meat of wild game like the bison and the buffalo. They used the furs and skins for clothing and blankets. They made shelters out of the hides. They used the bones to make tools and weapons like picks, spears, and knives. They also made tools out of wood and stone.

Minnie's people developed the *atl-atl* for hunting. To make an atl-atl they took a stick with a notch where the end of a spear could rest, giving more leverage. Using the atl-atl gave the hunters more powerful throws. They could hurl their spears or spear points farther with more force. The Paleoindians did not have the bow and arrow, but the atl-atl made hunting easier.

The earliest Paleoindian people used a flint spear point or dart point. The dart is now known as the Clovis fluted point. People coming later used a different dart point called the Folsom point. It was only about two inches long. Such points have been found from Alaska

Points found in a bonfire shelter in Val Verde, Texas. Institute of Texan Cultures illustration no. 70-24

▼▼▼

all the way to the Texas Gulf Coast. Clovis points have been found in the Llano Complex, a place on the high plains of West Texas, and in the hearths near Lewisville. Folsom points were also found on the plains of West Texas.

A third type of dart or spear point called the Plainview point has been found only on the plains. Wherever a site is discovered that contains any of the points, usually tools are also found. Such finds reinforce the idea that people have lived in Texas for a long time, and the fact that these sites have been found in many areas supports the theory that Paleoindians traveled in small groups as nomads.

In the Paleoindian culture, Minnie's people organized into small tribes or family clans numbering twenty to thirty people. They traveled and lived together. Larger groups found it difficult to move around and find enough food for everyone. When a group became too large, a couple of families would leave and form a new clan. The new clan lived independently of the older one, yet the related groups helped each other when they met.

Eventually some groups migrated great distances from the others. Over thousands of years, the different groups came to speak different languages. They developed different traditions and ways of living as they adapted to the land and climate. The Paleoindian era of Minnie's people lasted until about 8,000 B.C., or until about 10,000 years ago.

THE ARCHAIC ERA

About 8,000 B.C., the Paleoindian phase of human development in Texas changed. The early native peoples entered what scholars call the Archaic era, which lasted from approximately 8,000 B.C. to A.D. 800. The most notable characteristic of people of the Archaic age was that they drew on rocks, in caves, and on ledges. Scholars found several sites along the Rio Grande and Pecos River where people lived in rock shelters such as caves with overhangs. The overhangs

The American Buffalo

▼▼▼

The American buffalo originated in Asia and became one of the Old World species to cross the Bering land bridge in prehistoric times. The largest animal in North America, it could be found from Canada all the way to Mexico. Two kinds of buffalo survived into the modern age: the plains buffalo and the eastern woodlands buffalo.

The American buffalo has a hump over the front shoulders and a massive head with short, sharp horns. The mature bull or male stands seven feet tall, is twelve feet long and can weigh up to 2,400 pounds. The bull has a black beard about one foot long. The front part of the body is thickly covered with fur while the rear part has much shorter hair.

On the open plains, the buffalo gathered in

and ledges provided something like a porch. Caves remained cool in the hot summer and provided a shelter from rain or snowstorms. The people painted on the rocks and caves using twigs for brushes and a mixture of animal fat and rock dust for paint. The drawings on the cave walls showed important events from their lives. In the recent era, explorers found material artifacts such as nets, sandals, mats, and corncobs preserved from thousands of years ago. The rock shelters had remained dry, so the artifacts in the caves did not rot or fall apart.

Objects in the rock paintings suggest that the early Indians were religious. They believed that supernatural beings caused things to happen, both good and bad. The spirits might bring natural disasters like floods or tornadoes, illness and death, or predict the future.

The climate of Texas became hotter and dryer as cloud cover disappeared when many pools and lakes dried out as the Ice Age began to end. The climate of Texas became more like it is today. The climate change and the continued killing of animals by the Paleoindian people resulted in the "great extinctions." The large mammoths, giant bison, and other herds died off. Other animals such as the buffalos and deer became smaller in size.

In the Archaic Era, the people still hunted, but now they hunted smaller animals such as the woodland buffalo, which roamed from East Texas to Florida. The men also hunted bear, musk ox, moose, caribou, elk, mountain goats, deer, and smaller game using the atl-atl. During this period, the native peoples learned to construct the bow

American buffaloes grazing on the plains. Institute of Texan Cultures illustration no. 68-94

▼▼▼

A diorama of an Archaic Indian scene set in West Texas. Institute of Texan Cultures illustration no. 70-26

and arrow, which made it easier and safer to hunt. The gathering of food from trees and bushes remained the job of women and girls and became more important as the larger animals became extinct.

The people traveled less and lived in increasingly larger groups of extended families. Some Archaic peoples apparently settled in one place and became sedentary rather than nomadic. Scattered sites extend from near present-day El Paso to San Marcos and Corpus Christi. These old sites show that many of the earliest settlers lived in caves while others lived in brush shelters.

The Archaic peoples made other advances. They used a much larger collection of tools than did the Paleoindians. Stone tools often replaced the older bone tools. Archaic peoples had stone scrapers, axes, knives, choppers, picks, and drills. They also had stone mortars and pestles for grinding raw food into meal. They had flint darts, snares, traps, and stone pipes. Ornaments also were found. Craftsmen and craftswomen made polished stone pendants, beads, and pipes. They also used the native plants to weave mats, nets, and

herds. Females formed small groups. The young bulls stayed with the females while older bulls formed their own group within the band. In fall and spring, all the groups came together and roamed around, looking for food and water. Their grunts could be heard miles away. Sixty million buffaloes once roamed the present United States and provided for many needs of the native peoples.

By the 1860s, Americans and Europeans greatly valued buffalo fur. Professional hunters slaughtered the buffaloes to get the hides. This extermination of the buffaloes was seen by the U.S. government as a way to stop the movement of various Indian tribes and make them farmers confined to reservations. By the 1890s, the American buffaloes numbered less than 1,000 and were in danger of becoming extinct.

Indian Rock Art

▼▼▼

Rock art, or drawing on cave walls, has been found in more than 250 sites in Texas. The drawings include pictographs, paintings, and carvings made by prehistoric and historic Indians. The art has been found in caves and rock shelters along rivers and streams. Experts believe some of the rock art to be at least ten thousand years old.

The images drawn vary greatly. The variety suggests that people with different cultures did the artwork. Some paintings are eighteen feet tall while others are as small as one inch. The artists made their colors from powdered minerals mixed with animal fat. Red and black were the most common colors. But the artists also used brown, yellow, orange, and white.

At Hueco Tanks, forty miles east of El Paso, a pictograph shows Indians dancing. Institute of Texan Cultures illustration no. 73-310H

sandals. The Archaic peoples also tamed dogs, which were used for hauling their few possessions.[1]

Daily life revolved around the family. Most people continued to live in groups of extended kinship. They still traveled or settled together, and the roles of men and women remained different. The men continued to hunt, to fish, and to protect their families. Women still cared for children, prepared food, made clothes, and cared for the homes or shelters. Children learned their roles and life skills from their father and mother or other family members. These early people of the Archaic era became the mothers and fathers of the native peoples in Texas and all of the Americas.

Government remained simple. Elders made most decisions after talking with other members of the family or band. One older man might be seen as having special knowledge or skill and become the leader. But the elder consulted others before making important decisions.[2]

▼▼▼

THE WOODLAND ERA

Major changes took place between about 100 B.C. and A.D. 800. There was a major shift from the culture of hunting meat and gathering food to farming. As the people planted seeds for food their way of living changed from traveling with the hunt to settling in one place to tend the crops. This was the beginning of agriculture. Women receive the credit for the beginnings of farming in the Western Hemisphere. During the Archaic era, generations of women had closely observed Mother Nature in their role as gatherers. Indeed, in their religions, early Indians personified Mother Earth by creating and worshiping a goddess rather than a god.

The women and girls observed "God" most closely. They gathered all kinds of wild foods as they wandered far from the others, never knowing if they would locate enough food—until they began to plant seeds. They first learned to grow maize (corn). Originally a wild Mexican grass, corn became the first food staple of the native peoples.

To prepare corn, women simply boiled it or scraped the dried kernels off the cob to grind the kernels between stones to make meal-like flour. Boiling the corn meal with water made a mush, or the women added water to the meal and made a stiff dough, which they baked into bread. Of course, people ate ripe raw corn. American Indians grew maize more than 6,000 years before Spaniards brought the first wheat grain to the Americas in the 1500s.

Many peoples in the Woodland era worshiped corn because it was *the* basic food source. From the Red River Valley to the Rio Grande, Indians held frequent "corn dances." Dance rituals celebrated rainfall, the growing season, and the harvest. People with extra corn traded to other groups for such items as buffalo meat, hides, or pots.

The women also planted several varieties of beans. Together, corn, squash, and beans became known as the "American Triad." All native to the continent, these foods spread across the world once the first European explorers came to the Americas and took the foods and seeds with them back to Europe.

The art features many subjects including human figures and animals such as buffaloes and mountain lions. The early people drew trees, weapons, and sun symbols as well as different geometric shapes. Also included are maps and scenes of hunting and warfare. Some depict major events of tribal history. The artists also drew shamans or priests, which indicates the earliest Texans held religious beliefs.

Major sites of Indian rock art in Texas are found in caves at the junction of the Pecos River with the Rio Grande and at the junction of Devils River with the Rio Grande. Both sites are in Val Verde County and contain two of the largest collections of rock art in North America.

▼▼▼

To these early people, corn, beans, and squash represented fertility. Sometimes called the "three sisters," growers planted all three in the same mound. Bean roots provided a natural fertilizer while the corn stalks gave the beans a pole to climb. Squash grew around the base of the corn and bean plants, a practice that kept weeds from overwhelming the corn and beans.[3]

Other plants that Indian women began to grow in plots of land close to their shelters included pumpkins, tomatoes, peanuts, and onions, along with several kinds of fruit and tobacco. Today, the plants first gathered and planted by Indian women account for 60 percent of the world's agricultural wealth.

Once the people learned to grow crops, they had a more dependable source of food. But they had to stay in one place to cultivate the land, to protect the crops from wild animals and birds, and to harvest the foods. Many Indian bands or tribes gave up their nomadic ways and settled in one place. The time of the nomadic hunters and gatherers ended as some tribes settled and began farming. People became more social as they started living together in small villages. With abundant food supplies, small groups of people no longer had to split off from one another to avoid hunger. Instead, bigger, more stable communities came into being.

With a more reliable food supply and a settled lifestyle, the men did not have to spend as much time hunting. The men acquired new skills as flint knappers, workers in stone, traders, peacemakers, weavers, artists, warriors, and toolmakers. Some became priests, village leaders, or medicine men. In many groups the women still did most of the agricultural work. If women planted and tended crops, they "owned" the crops, achieving a higher status. Among men, they became more valued as wives. But in some tribes, men tended the fields.

As villages grew, trade among the villages increased. Trade then led to contact with different native peoples. They traded not only goods, but also ideas and practical knowledge. When different people meet they learn new ways from each other.

The Woodland era of Texas ended when the native people began planting small gardens, then larger plots, and finally fields. It was the

▼▼▼

beginning of agriculture. The people who adapted to agriculture and lived a settled life were called the "Neo-Indians," meaning new.[4]

Between A.D. 700 and A.D. 1500, the Mississippian Cultural Tradition developed. The culture spread westward from the Carolinas to East Texas. With surer food supplies, populations increased and villages got bigger. There was expanded trade and the sharing of ideas among the many tribal groups. Religious life became more complex, and increased learning about the natural world took place through mutual sharing as they traded.

Archaeologists discovered a pueblo culture along the Canadian River in West Texas. Remains indicate the people of the newly discovered culture lived much like the Pueblo Indians in what is now New Mexico and Arizona. They lived in apartment-styled adobe houses with stone walls around their settlements. These people came into Texas between the twelfth and thirteenth centuries where they worked the Alibates flint quarries and traded their flints for the goods of other tribes. Alibates flints have been found north to the Great Lakes, west to the Pacific coast, east to the Atlantic coast, and southeast to the coast of the Gulf of Mexico.

At the end of the fifteenth century the various people living in southern Texas knew the land from their centuries of following first the huge mammoths and then bison, with the men hunting using the atl-atl, then a spear tipped with flinthead, large clubs, and finally the bow and arrow. Those people living along the Gulf coast fished and collected shell foods. As they moved from place to place the women gathered various foods from the land. The coastal women also learned to gather seeds and plant them, just as Indian women elsewhere. Thus, the coastal women introduced an agricultural economy, which led some bands of the groups to settle down and begin farming. This in turn led to clustering of families into small villages usually located near a river to insure a supply of fresh water. There were established trading networks where the groups traded for goods and exchanged ideas. All the Texas native people had beliefs about spirits as well as stories passed on for generations about the beginnings of their people.

THE HISTORIC ERA

The Historic Era began in the early 1500s with the arrival of the strangers from countries in Europe. Some of these visitors left written records of their meetings with the native people. Five major native cultural groups lived in Texas at the time: the Caddo and the Wichita in the northeast; their neighbors, the Atakapan; the Coahuiltecan and Karankawa of South Texas; the Jumano in West Texas; and the Plains tribes.

The Caddo

Sometime after A.D. 500 and before A.D. 700, the Caddo coming from the eastern woodlands settled in the piney woods of East Texas and the land of western Louisiana. All the Caddo descended from native people in the Mississippi Valley. They were the westernmost branch of the Mississippi Tribal Culture and maintained a culture with complex social lives, large villages, and temple mounds. One Caddo tribe, the Hasinai, lived in East Texas. By 1100 they had built very large cities and towns throughout the area and were large-scale farmers. They settled in friendly groups with a chief along river valleys of eastern and northeastern Texas.

Another group, the Kadohadacho, lived in the Red River Valley near the borders of Texas-Louisiana-Arkansas. The third group, the Natchitoch, was located in Eastern Louisiana. The related tribes located within Texas included the Hasinai, the Neche, the Nacogdoche, the Nacono, the Kichai, and the Caddo proper. By the nineteenth century the twenty-five related groups became known as the Caddo. All maintained similar cultures.

One of the major Caddo colonies in Texas began along the Neches River Valley of East Texas, now called Cherokee County. The village located on a plain known as Mound Prairie had three mounds. The Caddo built stair-stepped, rectangular, flat-topped hills. The mounds puzzled scholars until they realized that the hills related to the Caddo religion. Atop the mounds, temples once existed along

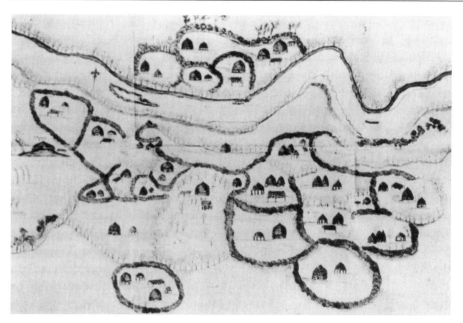

Map of Caddo village drawn in 1691 by Domingo de Teran. Institute of Texan Cultures illustration no. 68-47

with the homes of priests and important families. The Caddo built the tall curved structures out of mounds of cane and grass.

The mounds served as places of important ceremonies and rituals as well as burial sites for political and religious leaders. At Caddo Mounds, near Alto, Texas, three mounds and thirty burial pits were found that held about ninety individuals. The presence of such mass burial sites suggested that the early Caddo practiced human sacrifice or that massive deaths from disease had occurred.

The early Caddo structures made extensive use of materials found in the forests of East Texas. Tree branches furnished the frames for their lodges and temples. Bundles of cane provided roofing materials, which were then covered with grass to keep out the rain. The dome-shaped lodges resembled beehives or haystacks. The sixty-feet-wide by fifty-feet-high lodges provided housing for related families. The family continued as the most important social unit within each tribe.

The large Caddo towns had a well-developed political system. Each Caddo band had a hereditary chief called a *caddi*. The caddi kept order and settled the problems within each tribe. Sometimes towns banded together with several caddi answering to a *xinesí*, or

▼▼▼

high chief. The xinesí had responsibility for settling problems across tribal groups and was the top religious official. As religious leader he was in charge of overseeing the ceremonies as well as the continuous burning of the sacred fire. The xinesí inherited the job, claiming descent from the moon, and passed the position onto a son.

As a religious people the Caddo believed in one God, or Great Spirit, who created the world. Some called him Caddí-Ayo, meaning leader up above. They also believed in the devil called Caddaja, an ugly man with horns reaching toward the sky. Lesser spirits of the Caddo included their ancestors, other people, and animals. Natural events such as storms and clouds also had spirits, as did such objects as trees and rocks.

The Caddo also worshiped corn, Mother Earth, rain, and fire in their religion. Corn, necessary to feed the people, depended on earth, warmth, and rain to grow and required fire for cooking. Many Caddo ceremonies honored the spirits of Mother Earth, the Corn Goddess, and the Sacred Fire God.

The Caddo people had several legends to explain creation. Priests taught the people that the universe began with a woman and her two daughters. One daughter was a virgin; the other was pregnant. Caddaja, the devil, attacked and ate the pregnant daughter. The

Re-creation (c. 1988) of a Caddo shelter for family groups. Institute of Texan Cultures illustration no. 97-800

▼▼▼

An 1890 portrait of two Caddo chiefs. Institute of Texan Cultures illustration no. 89-131

mother and the surviving daughter went to the spot of the tragedy and grieved for the pregnant girl. They found a drop of the daughter's blood on an acorn shell. They took the shell home. In time, the acorn turned first into a little boy, then a man. After his grandmother equipped the man for war, he eventually killed Caddaja. When Caddaja died, the man, his grandmother, and his aunt flew to the sky where Cachao Ado, the man-god, ruled the heavens and the earth.

The Caddo legend about Zacado explains how planting and harvesting became part of the peoples' life. Zacado came up from the underworld with his wife. He brought a pipe filled with burning tobacco and his wife brought seeds for planting. Zacado and his wife taught the Caddo how to plant, cultivate, and harvest their crops. They worked large fields of beans, squash, pumpkins, corn, sunflowers, and other crops. The Caddo also had orchards of peach, plum, fig, and chestnut trees. Other groups of people brought the peaches and figs to the region. The Caddo became skilled farmers.

Gender determined work duties. Women harvested wild foods like fruits, berries, grapes, rice, and onions. They learned the best ways to cook the food provided by nature. To make bitter acorn nuts eatable, they shelled them and ground the nutmeat into meal. Next, they soaked the meal in water, removing some of the bitter taste, and then dried it. Once dried, the acorn meal could be used in making a soup, mush, or bread. Women also dried food and buried it to keep cool for use during the winter when food became scarce. Each clan or band also distributed extra food throughout the Caddo villages to insure that all their kinsmen had enough food during the cold winter months. Women produced about 50 percent of the food eaten by their people.

As in earlier cultures, the men and boys protected their clan or tribe from hostile people; they hunted and fished; they did most of the lodge building; they made their tools and moccasins; and they helped the women harvest. When trading with other peoples, some Caddo men functioned as merchant-diplomats.

Potters made clay containers using a coiling technique for holding foods. They also made bottles, jars, bowls, cups, and other vessels

Caddo Henry Edge in traditional dress. Institute of Texan Cultures illustration no. 68-48

of clay. Some potters made small human or animal figures. The Caddo used small figurines in religious rituals and other figurines for children's toys. Pottery items included long-stemmed smoking pipes and beads for personal adornment. Potters with artistic talents painted their work with geometric patterns similar to those of the Aztecs.

Caddo women gathered plants and herbs with healing properties. They also tanned and decorated animal hides for use as blankets and clothing. They cut hides into strips to use as ropes and lashing materials. The men fashioned animal bones into tools and personal items like hairpins and combs. The Caddo also traded for buffalo skins that they used for boat coverings as well as for other purposes.

A vast trade network existed among the early tribes. The Caddo villages in the Neches Valley were major regional trade centers. The Caddo traded with the Jumano tribes who lived west of the Pecos River. The Caddos received turquoise ornaments and woven cotton cloth for use as clothing and blankets. They also bartered or exchanged goods with the Comanche and Kiowa of the West Texas plains. The Caddos offered their lances, shields, pottery, baskets, mats, and drums. In return, they received buffalo meat and hides from the Plains tribes.

But by A.D. 1100, the settlement at Caddo Mounds near the Neches River went into decline. The Caddo abandoned the Neches River site altogether by 1300, but the Caddo culture survived because their villages had developed over such a wide area. During the late Caddo era, from 1300 to 1800, the Caddos continued to build mounds, but they were smaller and further apart. The far-reaching trade patterns collapsed with local trade routes replacing them.

When the first Europeans arrived in 1542 they still found a well-developed and self-sufficient culture based on a village lifestyle that relied on the extensive farming of corn and other foods. They had a complex system of authority, ritual, and ceremonies as well as status ranks within the social groups. But the Europeans spread war and fatal diseases among the Caddos. For example, in July, 1542, about

A Caddo clay pipe recovered from site at Toledo Bend Reservoir. Institute of Texan Cultures illustration no. 68-44

three hundred men with Hernando de Soto on a gold hunting expedition entered the area between the Angelina and Neches Rivers where one group of the Caddo, the Hasinai, lived, and caused much destruction. The Caddos also fell victim to the more aggressive raiding tribes from the plains country.[5] In later years the government moved many of the Caddo tribal groups into Indian Territory, now western Oklahoma.

The Atakapa

Until the early 1800s, the Atakapas lived southeast of the Caddo along the Louisiana-Texas border to around Galveston. The word "Atakapa" comes from the Choctaw language and meant "eaters of men." As a small group of related people, their major tribes included the Atakapa proper, the Bidais, and a couple of others. In Texas, their major settlements developed along the lower Neches River Valley. Archeologists working in the Houston-Galveston area found several Atakapa sites. The archeologists believe that the Atakapa settlements date to about the time of Christ.

The Atakapas lived as fishermen, hunters, and gatherers who

did not farm. Using simple brushwood traps, the fishermen caught all types of marine life from turtles to flounder and oysters to clams. They hunted deer, bear, and, sometimes, buffalo. For additional meat the hunters snared small game like rabbits and prairie chickens using traps made of cane. Each year, most Atakapas moved westward for an annual buffalo hunt. But the Atakapas got their best supply of meat, oils, and hides from alligators. They used the oil as repellent against mosquitoes, the hides for clothing and as material for shelter coverings. They lived in portable brush huts easily built as they moved from place to place gathering food.

When spearing fish or hunting in coastal bays and lagoons, Atakapas used "dugout" canoes made of tree trunks cut in half and hollowed out. From forty to fifty feet long, one canoe could hold an entire family and their few possessions. However, the clumsy and hard-to-maneuver craft could not be used in the deep gulf waters, so the Atakapas limited their fishing to the inlets and bays along the coast.

Scholars know little about the culture of the Atakapas except that they adopted some Caddoan ways such as tattooing their bodies as well as using body paint. The men wore long breechclouts or went naked, and women wore skirts of Spanish moss and grasses or animal hides. In ceremonies, the Atakapa men danced while the women sang. Dance rituals typically lasted three days and nights.

Larger groups of Atakapas organized into independent bands of close relatives. Each band had a chief, a wise tribal elder who made important decisions. He kept law and order and settled disputes among members of the band. When conflicts erupted between bands the chiefs met and negotiated until they solved the problem.

Like some other tribes, the Atakapa kept slaves. Simars de Bellisle, a Frenchman, was marooned near Galveston when his ship sailed off course in 1720. The Atakapa found him near death. Stripped of his clothes and possessions he was made a slave of the Atakapa for over a year. As a slave he did women's work: hauling wood and water and gathering food.

The Atakapas were described as a short, muscular people with dark skin and sloping foreheads. In infancy, the mother tied a thin board to the baby's forehead, leaving it there until the forehead formed into the desired slant. They used bark for their infants' cradleboards and Spanish moss gathered from trees for diapers.

The Atakapas' creation story told that they came out of the sea. Large oyster shells contained human life. From the oyster shells they grew first into children and then adults. The Atakapas also believed that a great flood occurred long ago. The flood waters swallowed men, women, children, animals, and many man-made structures. Only people living in the mountains survived.

The Atakapas believed in an afterlife. People eaten by their enemies or who died from snakebite would not join the afterlife of the spirits. This belief was probably the reason the Atakapas sometimes cooked and ate body parts of their enemies. They could take revenge and further punish an enemy through this ritual cannibalism. This was a common belief and practice among several of the Texas tribes.

The coming of the Europeans eventually spelled the end of the Atakapa, who died of epidemic diseases. About 1700, the Atakapa population was approximately 3,500, but by 1800 their number was only 175, and most of the group lived in Louisiana. In 1908, only nine people claimed descent from the Atakapa tribes.

The Bidais, a subtribe of the Akakapas, lived in Southeast Texas along the lower Neches and Trinity Rivers. The Caddos and the Bidais shared land. Although the Bidais adopted many Caddo ways, they did not farm like the Caddo. The Bidais lived as hunters and gatherers and generally had a difficult existence finding enough food.

The Bidai also became victims of European diseases. A single epidemic in 1776–77 killed about 50 percent of their group. Those remaining merged with other Atakapa bands. By 1860, the few remaining Bidai were forced by white settlers into Indian Territory, where they lost their distinct identity as a tribe.[6]

The Karankawa

The Karankawas lived from Galveston Bay southwest to Corpus Christi Bay. The Coahuiltecans, a group of about two hundred subtribes or bands, lived south of the Karankawas and deep into Mexico. A common language united the two groups.

The Karankawas first encountered Europeans in 1528 when Spanish survivors of a shipwreck washed ashore just west of Galveston Island where the Karankawas roamed. Cabeza de Vaca led the group, and they lived among the Karankawas for almost six years.

Karankawa warriors stood more than six feet tall, much taller than Indians from other tribes. European reports described them as powerful runners and swimmers. Both men and women painted and tattooed their bodies. They made cuts into their face, hands, arms, and chests using strong, sharp cactus thorns. Then they mixed a charcoal of walnut wood, crushed and soaked in water, and smeared the mixture into the cuts. The charcoal ink formed permanent marks in the skin. They also pierced their lower lips and breasts. They placed small pieces of cane in the pierced holes to look more attractive and beautiful.

An 1888 drawing of Texas coastal Indians that could be Karankawas or Coahuiltecans. Institute of Texan Cultures illustration no. 75-23

▼▼▼

28

The word "Karankawas" originally meant "dog-lovers" or "dog-raisers." They kept dogs that looked like the fox or the coyote and roamed a hostile, marshy, and brush environment, apparently being pushed into the region by more aggressive tribes. The winters could be cold with hot and dry summers. The desertlike area inland from the Gulf coast had few trees, but cactus and brushy plants were plentiful.

Living in an area unfit for agriculture, these native people lived as hunters and gatherers. They traveled in small family groups and roamed the brush country searching for food. Large groups found it difficult to find enough food for everyone, so they remained in small groups and moved frequently.

The men made bows almost as tall as they were. Made from red cedar, the longbow propelled the arrows farther and with more force than shorter bows. They made the arrows out of slender shoots of cane. Using their bows and arrows, they hunted for deer, javelina, wild turkeys, ducks, and alligators while trapping smaller game like rabbits, frogs, snakes, and rats. The women gathered fruit, nuts, berries, and other plant food such as prickly pears and wild onions. When other foods got scarce, they also caught and ate insects.

When along riverbanks or coastline, they fished and dug for oysters, clams, and scallops. Like the Atakapas, they traveled in rough dugout canoes to the coastal inlets and nearby islands and harvested the foods available there. The Karankawas also used their canoes to raid other tribes; they attacked their enemies using the longbow and arrows while hidden in the marshy grasses along the river inlets and coastal banks.

The Karankawas practiced ritual cannibalism. They cooked and ate parts of captured enemy chiefs or warriors. They believed that they acquired the magical powers and courage of their dead enemies if they ate them. They used cannibalism as part of their rituals and ceremonies but rarely as a primary source of food.

They lived in portable huts made by using willow poles that they bent for a frame and covered with animal skins, leaves, and branches. They lined pottery and baskets with natural tar found on the Gulf Coast beaches to make them hold water.

The Karankawas gave their children two names. One name they used in "public" and the other was a secret name with magical powers. Only close family members knew the secret name.

Composed of small traveling bands, the organization of the Karankawas remained simple. Minor chiefs presided over the many different nomadic bands and kept order within the groups. The Karankawas believed in two major gods, Mel and Pichini, and worshiped many lesser spirits or gods.

The Coahuiltecans

The Coahuiltecans also lived in small bands much like the Karankawas but traveled a much wider area of South Texas. Coahuiltecan bands included the Payayas who lived around today's San Antonio; the Aranamas who traveled southeast of the Payayas; the Orejones who lived farther south of the Aranama; and numerous other bands. All these groups were communal; they shared their food and goods equally. Like the Karankawas, they traveled with few possessions searching for food as hunters and gatherers who had adapted to the harsh, dry climate of the area.

In 1689 the Alonso de León expedition traveling north from Mexico found Jean Géry, a deserter from the earlier La Salle expedition, where he lived as a leader among the Coahuiltecans along the Rio Grande. He lived in a shelter covered with buffalo skins, his lodge secured by over forty warriors with bows and arrows.[7] The Coahuiltecans lived in shelters made from a frame of poles covered with woven mats and animal hides. They wove baskets, mats, and nets from dried plant fibers and used nets as carrying bags as well as for fishing.

Finding enough food was their primary concern. Wild plants such as the bulb of the agave plant, the prickly pear fruit, and mesquite bean made up their basic foods along with pecans and acorns. Women ground both the mesquite beans and agave bulbs into nutritious flour. The Indians squeezed and drank the juice from the prickly pear fruit, which they made into an alcoholic drink. They skinned and ate the young, tender pads of the prickly pears as well as dried them to store for use when food was scarce. When food could not be found, they mixed ground up wood and dirt with what food they had to make the food bulkier and shared with all.

The men hunted with their bows and arrows, wooden lances, and wooden or bone knives. Wild game included deer, javelina, and an occasional buffalo or bear. Hunters also killed rabbits, rats, mice, ducks, lizards, frogs, and armadillos. When food became especially scarce, the Coahuiltecans ate ant eggs and rotten wood. The men also fished in the rivers and streams. After the Europeans came into the area, the Coahuiltecans developed livestock herds and did less hunting.

During the warm months, the men usually went without body coverings, but the women covered themselves with deerskin skirts. In very cold weather, both men and women usually wore rabbit-skin robes. As they traveled, they made temporary housing by placing reed mats over tiny trees, which created a low, small, circular shelter.

A "headman" provided the leadership for each band of Coahuiltecans. He was someone who had achieved fame as a great hunter or warrior or both. With limited power, the headman had to keep the loyalty of his warriors or the unhappy warriors would leave to join another band. To retain loyalty, most headmen were generous men who put the safety and well being of the band first. The comfort of the band came next. Often, after a communal hunt, he waited until all received their food before he as headman got some for himself. Such deeds proved to the members of the band that the unselfish headman put his followers ahead of himself.

Coahuiltecan society had three characteristics: All in the band were related; they functioned as equals with no social or economic classes; and the people remained with the group as long as they did not hurt their relatives or neighbors. Within the tribal group they cooperated in such work as putting up their shelters and defending their territory.

The Coahuiltecans believed that supernatural spirits controlled

▼▼▼

the world and provided everything. The spirits gave rain and good harvests of prickly pears. The spirits kept people well or made them sick. The people related to the spirit world through their shamans who went into trances and entered the world of the spirits, communicated with them, and returned. The shamans functioned as both healers and interpreters of the spirit world.

The *mitote* ceremony took place among the Coahuiltecans as a thanksgiving for good fortune. It might occur when a boy killed his first deer and thus became a man or when a girl became a woman. The mitote celebration also took place after winning a battle against enemies. The ceremony included an all-night feast and dance with lots of merriment. After dark, women roasted meat over a large fire, and the music from drums and gourd rattles began. As the meat cooked, all the people danced in a circle around the fire. The dance continued all night, even while eating. Some dancers took peyote, a natural drug that induced visions. While in a trance, some participants talked with the Great Spirit.

The entertainment for the men and boys included several games. They had wrestling matches, foot races, several kinds of ball games, and target competitions with arrows, knives, and spears.

By custom, the Coahuiltecans isolated and abandoned their sick. Sick people had to take care of themselves. In one case, when a man had smallpox, others propped him against a tree using brambles to keep him in an upright position. Tribal members believed that keeping him upright prevented the spirit that infected him from leaving his body and infecting someone else.

While shorter than the Karankawa, the Coahuiltecans also painted and tattooed their faces and bodies. Each band or tribe had different tattoo designs and could be identified by them. Both sexes wore their hair long, down to their waists. They also pierced their ears, noses, and breasts and inserted feathers, sticks, and bones into the holes for ornamentation.

Both the Karankawas and the Coahuiltecans experienced declines in their population after the Spaniards came. Diseases killed great numbers of them. Spanish colonists often pushed them off the best land. Periodically, the Indians rebelled, but Spaniards crushed all such attempts to overthrow their rule. Deadly raids of the Comanches and Apaches killed many. Both the Coahuiltecans and the Karankawas ceased to exist as cultural groups about the 1850s.[8]

The Jumano

The Jumano lived in three geographical areas: New Mexico, Nueva Vizcaya, and West Texas. Between 1535 and 1684 numerous European explorers, friars, and soldiers encountered people that came to be called the Jumano. European explorers and leaders of expeditions such as Álvar Núñez Cabeza de Vaca, Hernán Gallegos, Juan de Oñate, Vicente de Zaldívar, and Francisco Vasquéz de Coronado all met groups spread over a broad area who are thought to have been Jumano.

Although little is known about the Jumano, at the beginning of the 1500s fifteen villages existed in the valleys of the Rio Grande. The villages spread from present-day El Paso down the Rio Grande as far as today's Presidio. Living a settled lifestyle on farms, the Jumano produced lots of different vegetables including corn, squash, several varieties of beans, and pumpkins. They also grew some tobacco. Related to the Pueblo people of New Mexico and Arizona, they developed a similar lifestyle. They lived along the river in flat-roofed adobe or dried mud houses clustered in large pueblos headed by chiefs who settled problems that arose. Portions of the homes or ceremonial chambers were underground.

Other western and central bands of the Jumano adopted a seminomadic lifestyle. Their way of life relied heavily on the buffalo. They traveled across the West Texas plains hunting buffalo.

The Jumano were strong and had painted or tattooed strips on their faces. Women wore their hair long; men cut theirs short to the middle of head; then they curled the remainder into a bun, leaving a lock of hair at the crown to which they attached feathers.[9]

The Jumano practiced many rituals and ceremonies and particularly loved music. At harvest time, the tribe celebrated by building a

▼▼▼

huge bonfire. Then, some would sing and clap their hands. Others danced around the bonfire and kept "time" to the music. The men usually dressed in buffalo robes while the women and girls wore deerskin clothing.

As early as 1200, the Jumano tribe lived in an important location and was part of a large trade network that included the Caddo in East Texas and the Pueblo Indians in New Mexico. With Jumano groups along the Rio Grande and north into Central Texas, they connected most of the Indian people of Texas into a vast trade network. The Jumano traded corn, beans, buffalo meat, and pottery for cotton blankets and nuggets of turquoise. With the Spanish expeditions came new plants such as peaches and melons and animals such as sheep and horses, which also found their way into the trading network of the Jumano.

As bands of Apache began moving south in the 1600s the Jumano entered a decline by the 1700s. During the next one hundred years the Jumano tried to get Spanish help to stop the disruption of their trade networks and villages. But eventually many Jumano fled southward to live as Mexican peasants working on Spanish haciendas while others joined various Apache groups. Over the years and with their trade routes broken this vast tribe disintegrated and ceased to exist as a distinct tribe in Texas.[10]

The Plains Indians

In West Texas, the Southern Plains Indians represented another cultural group. The group included the Comanche, Kiowa, Apache, Kiowa Apache, Lipan Apache, Mescalero Apache, and Tonkawa. Before the introduction of the horse, the tribes moved around the Great Plains on foot with dogs pulling their household goods on *travoises*.

After acquiring the horse, all the Plains tribes followed the buffalo herds. The buffalo supplied their major needs. They ate the meat and used the hides for clothing and blankets. They built tipis using the hides to cover long, pine-pole frames. They made tools and weapons

▼▼▼

The Jumano women used a rock hole to crush and grind their grain into meal. These grinding holes are located west of Fort Davis. Institute of Texan Cultures illustration no. 73-312A

out of the bones. They fashioned ropes and lashings from buffalo sinews, the muscle strands. Stomach pouches became storage bags. They even melted the buffalo fat and drank it. In addition to the buffalo, the men also hunted antelope, deer, turkey, and other wild game.

In the Plains tribes, groups of families or clans were the major social and political units. Family groups formed bands headed by a

▼▼▼

chief. Chiefs in turn formed temporary alliances with other bands and tribes for common purposes including warfare or organized hunting parties. The Comanche councils comprised all men and all participated in making decisions. The council recognized men as peace and war chiefs, but they remained in the position only as long as the others supported them.

Warriors raided other tribal bands, stealing food and goods as needed. Yet, within their own tribe, they obeyed stern rules of conduct. The rules or laws had to be obeyed because any tribal member could condemn a person and possibly send a lawbreaker into exile. They also had a code of honor when dealing with allies.

All of these tribal groups had important social ceremonies or rituals. One custom related to an older man. He could become a shaman who was also a medicine man, or healer, if he had supernatural experiences and visions. He performed ceremonies to bring good luck to his band or tribe.

All Plains tribes valued children. A ceremony was conducted to welcome an older girl into the women's society of the tribe. Adults built the girl a lodge where, dressed all in white, she received guests and accepted many presents. The adults believed that the girl-woman could grant special blessings and bring the tribe good luck. After a four-day celebration, the woman-girl could marry.

The men, of course, valued boys more than girls, because the young males could become hunters and warriors. Another ceremony involved teenaged boys around age sixteen. Generally, a boy's uncles trained him as a warrior and taught him to hunt. The boy then accompanied warriors on four raids or hunts. If the boy did well, adult warriors let everyone know that the boy was now a man. Afterward, the man-boy was free to marry and to join the men on their hunts or raids. The Kiowas had a school for boys: the Rabbit Society. All Kiowa boys automatically became members. Two men instructed the Rabbits and drilled them in the skills needed by a great hunter-warrior. Elders gave each Rabbit-boy a piece of elk hide to wear on the back of his head. All boys realized the honor of this ritual, but to continue wearing the elk hide, the Rabbits had to act like men. As

A Kiowa mother with her children posing for a studio portrait, c. 1890. Institute of Texan Cultures illustration no. 89-127

they grew older, the Rabbits gained more and more responsibilities until they became full-fledged warriors. Special religious ceremonies, festive celebrations, and feasts were held in the Rabbit Society. In one dance, they hopped and jumped like rabbits.

Just as boys became members of the Rabbit Society, the warriors had different military societies called "dog soldiers." The most important and prestigious society was the Koitsenko. By election, only ten of the greatest, most respected warriors could belong to the Koitsenko.

The dark-skinned Kiowas of the Plains were short and stocky with thick chests. Warriors cut their hair short on the right side, which showed their ear ornaments. On the left side, the hair grew long for braiding into a scalp-lock. Women simply parted their hair in the middle and made two braids. Alternately, some women wore a headband and allowed their hair to hang loose. Both men and women wore tattoos and some women painted small circles on their foreheads.

The Kiowas believed that one all-powerful God created the world and everything in it, except the Kiowas. The Creator traveled westward until He found a hollow tree. He gave the hollow tree a tremendous blow, and out came the Kiowas as grown men and women. On a second blow, more adults came out. With the third blow, children came forth, and the Kiowa Nation was formed.

The Kiowas did not worship the sun but respected its role in the seasons. Their most important ritual, although named the Sun Dance, celebrated the return of the buffalo to their hunting grounds. All the Kiowa bands came together and camped in a circle for the ceremonial dance. The Kiowa's most sacred item was the Tai-me, a small green stone carved into a human likeness. Its makers dressed the carved stone in a robe of white feathers and a headdress made of tobacco leaves. For the tribe, the Tai-me represented the source of spiritual power.[11]

Another sacred object included the "ten grandmothers" that the Kiowas kept in medicine bundles. The legend tells about a male child named Tah'lee, who was born from the union of the sun and a Kiowa woman. The Great Spirit divided the Tah'lee into ten medicines called the "ten grandmothers." The medicine bundle containing the "ten grandmothers" was opened in secret by the medicine man, who used them in a special annual ceremony.

The Kiowa buried their dead in caves or between rocks, piling rocks and earth over the body, which they wrapped in blankets, and clothing. Their custom was to place every article belonging to the person in the grave and often their ponies and dogs were also killed. . . . This was done because they [relatives] did not want to see these things that belonged to their dead. The Kiowas believed that there was a place of peace and happiness to which the good would go after death, [and] also a place of punishment to which the evil would be consigned by the Great Spirit.[12]

Both the nomadic and the settled ways of the Texas Indians changed forever as European expeditions came to the area. Among all the Indian cultural groups, major changes took place in the next four centuries. When Columbus arrived in the West Indies in 1492 at least twelve million native people lived in present-day Canada and the United States. Some experts set the number as high as twenty-five million. Another thirty-five million Indians lived in Central America and sixty million or so lived in South America. But Europeans, and later Americans, brought war and diseases that reduced the millions to merely thousands.

Europeans who followed Columbus eventually destroyed the way of life of the native people. The European and American invasions into the land of the various Indian tribes changed the native people of Texas forever.

CHAPTER 2

The Invasions of the Europeans and Americans

OVER TIME, Indian lands were invaded by outsiders. Such contacts were lengthy and complex. Ultimately, the outsiders would destroy the Indians of Texas.

THE SPANISH INVASION

The first European encounters with the native peoples of Texas were with the coastal tribes in 1528. A few stragglers from the failed military expedition of Panfilo de Narváez were shipwrecked in Florida. After making crude boats they sailed from Florida along the Gulf Coast in an effort to reach Mexico. But another storm washed them ashore west of Galveston Island.

THE KARANKAWAS

Karankawas met the Spanish survivors on Galveston Island with awe and delight in seeing the strange people. They held a welcome ceremony complete with dancing, gift giving, and food. Later, the Spaniards tried to make another raftlike boat to get to Mexico, but the boat quickly sank. The strange white men lost most of their armor, weapons, and clothes, and the Karankawas' delight turned to contempt because the strangers now had nothing of value to give them.

Showing their contempt, the Karankawas captured and enslaved Álvar Núñez Cabeza de Vaca, Estevanico, and several others in 1528. At first, the Spaniards were worked like brutes by the Indians, but as the days and months went by, Cabeza de Vaca impressed the Karankawas with his healing powers. His treatment consisted of blessing the ill person, breathing on any injuries, and praying. De Vaca became a respected medicine man in one of the bands. As de Vaca moved from place to place with the Karankawas, he also traded with other groups, including the Coahuiltecans.

Cabeza de Vaca left a written account about his time with the Karankawas and Coahuiltecans. He noted the great endurance of the Coahuiltecans as they could chase a deer all day without rest. Also noted was their skill with bows and arrows. When they hunted, the men used the "surround" method where the adult men and boys encircled a herd of animals. Then the hunters moved in together to make their kills. They also set bushes and logs on fire to force game to move in the direction that the hunters desired.

De Vaca wrote of the Karankawas' body adornment. Men and women painted and tattooed their bodies. They also painted and tattooed any slave or enemy they captured. Designs on their bodies included representations of animals, birds, flowers, or other natural scenes. He additionally commented on the piercing of the lower lip and breast nipple with pieces of cane inserted. De Vaca hinted that he found the women attractive and that the children were well loved. The children nursed until about twelve years of age to insure sufficient food to make them grow strong. Women wore skirts of deerskin or Spanish moss while the men remained unclothed most of the time except when cold weather came. Even in winter with snow and ice all around, men took baths in a pool or stream after breaking the ice. De Vaca wrote that they mainly ate fish, oysters, and other food from the Gulf waters. De Vaca and his three men left the coastal area in 1534. They wandered to the west and south, meeting other native tribes, and eventually reached Mexico City.

▼▼▼

By the 1540s, Spanish slave traders sailed along the coast and kidnapped Karankawas. Using force or trickery, the slave traders captured them and sold them into slavery. By the 1860s, only a handful of Karankawas remained. They moved into Mexico and settled near San Fernando in Tamaulipas. After experiencing attacks in Mexico, they returned to Texas and settled in Rio Grande City where the last group died out.[1]

Unknowingly, the Spanish also introduced foreign diseases to the native people they encountered. The native people had no immunity or resistance to European diseases. The deadliest diseases included smallpox, cholera, measles, chicken pox, and mumps. Diseased Indians spread illness and death to other tribes as they traveled and traded. Between 1528 and 1890, more than thirty major epidemics killed an estimated 95 percent of all the native peoples in Texas.

> Three thousand East Texas Caddos died from some unknown disease in 1691. Smallpox virtually wiped out the Coahuiltecan Indians living in the Rio Grande missions in 1706. The Caddos got hit again in 1718, and more than 100 people died if not more. Smallpox and measles killed off most of the Indians in the five San Antonio missions in 1739. Sometime before 1746, smallpox and measles devastated the Tonkawas and Atakapas. Smallpox hit them again in 1750 as well as those living in the San Xavier missions. . . . Malaria and dysentery got the San Xavier missions and the Tonkawas and Atakapas in 1753. Smallpox and measles hit the Hasinai in 1759. Half the population of the San Antonio missions died in 1763.[2]

The Indians of East Texas also had a disastrous experience when survivors of the Hernando de Soto expedition came through Texas. De Soto's men hacked their way across the land from Florida and killed men, women, and children as they moved toward Mexico. Spaniards looted and burned scores of native villages while spreading the killer diseases. Experts believe that the Caddo they encountered had a population of about 200,000 in 1500. Then European

▼▼▼

diseases began to kill off the Caddo. By 1600, specialists believe that the native population was reduced to somewhere between 8,000 and 40,000 people.

Depopulation brought cultural death for some clans and groups. Ancestral traditions were lost when an entire group died off or when a fragment of a band merged with other bands or tribes. The men and women who transferred their culture to later generations were lost. Singers, dancers, interpreters, medicine men and women, crafts people, and others who would have passed on their culture died.[3]

THE HORSE

The early meetings with the Europeans brought disease and death to the native Texans. But the Europeans also brought the horse, the animal that changed the Indian way of life forever. The native people of Texas first acquired horses from the numerous Spanish expeditions as the soldiers and friars came north into the Texas territory, then a part of New Spain. Scholars argue about the exact dates, but current evidence indicates that the native peoples probably got their first horses in the early years of the seventeenth century from the conquistador Juan de Oñate.

Oñate led Spanish colonists into present-day New Mexico and founded Santa Fe in 1609. It became the capital of Oñate's province. Soon, prosperous farms and ranches dotted the area. In the new colony, Oñate used the Pueblo people as slaves to haul wood, cook, and perform other chores of daily life. Along with their other work, the Pueblo men cared for Oñate's horses. Upon seeing horses for the first time, some Indians called them "wonder dogs" or "magic dogs." Though not permitted to mount the horses, some Indians managed to escape from the Spaniards, sometimes on horseback. Soon, other tribal groups came in contact with the new animals called horses.

By 1659, the Apaches had horses. They learned to use them in lightning-fast raids against the Spanish settlements in today's New Mexico, where they captured more horses. The horse proved especially beneficial to the other Plains people like the Comanche, Kiowa, and Kiowa Apache, all tribes living and moving around West Texas. The flat, treeless plains provided a natural grazing area for horses. As tribes moved, the horse culture spread to other tribes. The Jumano of western Texas acquired horses. Even the Caddo in East Texas had horses by the mid-1680s.

The horse created a more dependable life for the Texas tribes, but the animal also changed the culture of the Native Americans. They could eat the animals in times of hunger, but the horse was more valuable alive. The horse allowed them to travel greater distances faster when hunting buffalo. Tipis could be made bigger because now the horse rather than the dog would drag the poles weighted with heavier loads of buffalo skins.

The horse also changed the nature of Indian warfare. Aggressive tribes became even more assertive. Blood feuds among tribes increased in number. With such mobility and speed raiders seemed to appear from nowhere, capture people, take their possessions, and quickly disappear. Just one warrior on horseback could create chaos, disrupt an enemy village, or change the course of a battle, if the warrior had enough courage.

Even settled Indians like the Caddo made good use of their horses. Riding a horse proved much better than walking. In addition, many Caddo tribes had an annual hunt. At least once each year, they went west to kill buffalo, and the horse made the chase easier.

Horses became a valued trade item. The tribal societies bestowed much honor upon a successful, fearless warrior with many horses. Such a warrior might even become a chief, especially in tribes like the Apache, Wichita, Comanche, and Kiowa. The peaceful Caddo also respected a good fighter who had lots of horses.[4]

With the horse, though, came the European soldiers looking for wealth and priests who tried to convert the people to Christianity. But the Spaniards found no great wealth and few Indians could be enticed to accept the God of the strangers. So the Spaniards lost interest in their northern lands of Texas.

THE FRENCH INVASION

Meanwhile, the native people of Texas were destined to become part of an international power struggle occurring in Europe, a struggle that eventually involved Spaniards, Frenchmen, and, much later, Americans.[5] Spanish interest in Texas revived when Spaniards learned of a French settlement in Texas. The Spanish sent several land and sea expeditions to search for the French enemy settlement.

In 1684, the French explorer René Robert Cavelier, Sieur de La Salle, founded a settlement. He led a group of priests, colonists, and soldiers who intended to establish a trading post and settlement at the mouth of the Mississippi. La Salle's ships inadvertently sailed past the Mississippi and were shipwrecked at Matagorda Bay.

As an experienced explorer La Salle, along with his Shawnee companion Nika, spoke several native languages. One exploring party of La Salle's encountered the Karankawa. The Karankawa were initially friendly until La Salle stole a couple of their canoes. Using their bows and arrows, the Karankawas killed two Frenchmen and wounded numerous others. Repelling several attacks over the months, La Salle and his entourage hauled supplies into the land of the Karankawas and founded Fort St. Louis at Garcitas Creek.

La Salle's colonists struggled from the beginning. They eventually negotiated with the Karankawa, trading some of their limited supplies for food and more canoes. La Salle even had his men build a canoe. They first made a frame of wooden bars. Then they sewed together strips of buffalo hides, stretched the hides over the frame, and greased the seams with a concoction of buffalo fat and charcoal to make the canoe watertight. The canoe was portable; it could be dismantled and reassembled as needed.

La Salle led several small expeditions into the interior of Texas, where several of his men deserted and joined various tribal bands. He made two trips northward where he encountered the Cenis or Tejas Indians, a group of the Caddo. On the first trip in 1686, he traded presents with leaders, giving metal knives to the men and glass beads to the women. When La Salle left the friendly natives returning to Fort St. Louis, he was loaded with all the corn meal, beans, and other provisions that his few horses could carry.

The next year, La Salle made a second trip to see the Tejas. Along the way, he and his men also visited other Caddo tribes. The Frenchmen traded with all of them. One trade exchanged metal needles for a superb, finely dressed, snow-white deerskin. Then the Frenchman showed the Indians how to sew using needles, a skill that spread to many Indian bands and tribes. The people continued to show their friendship by provisioning the French party. Indians gave them corn, meal, beans, nut meats, sunflower seeds, along with some buffalo skins.

A friend of La Salle, Henri Joutel, kept a detailed journal of the French expedition to Texas, from 1684 to 1687. While in the Caddo village, a war party left to attack the tribe's Indian enemies to the west. Several Frenchmen joined the war party. After the raid, Joutel wrote the following account:

> I believe I have spoken elsewhere of this practice of taking scalps. It involves cutting the skin all around the head down to the ears and forehead. They then lift the entire skin, which they take great care to clean and to preserve and display in their huts. They thus leave the sufferer with an exposed skull. . . . The warriors brought another woman [captive]. . . . Then they gave [her] to the [Cenis tribe of the Caddo] women and girls. . . . They armed themselves, some with short heavy sticks, others with wooden skewers they had sharpened. . . . The unfortunate woman could do nothing but await the finishing stroke, suffering as it were the martyr's role, for one tore away a handful of hair, another cut off a finger, another dug out an eye. Each one made a point of torturing her in some way; and in the end there was one who struck a hard blow to her head and another who drove a skewer into her body. After that she died, they then cut her up into several pieces, which the victors carried with them, and they forced several other slaves [captives] taken earlier to eat the pieces.[6]

▼▼▼

News of the French colony in the Spanish-claimed territory alarmed Spanish authorities, who sent expeditions searching for their enemy. In 1690, Alonso de León on one of his many trips led Fray Damián Massanet to East Texas, the homeland of the Caddos. Massanet wanted to build missions and Christianize the Indians.

On their way de León's expedition found Jean Géry, a sailor who deserted from La Salle. Géry had become the leader of a band of the Coahuiltecans living twenty leagues from the Rio Grande. Géry received de León sitting in a buffalo-skin shelter and a chair of skins guarded by warriors.

With the Cenis branch of the Caddo, the Spaniards also found two young boys left behind by La Salle's party to learn the Caddo language and how to live in the Texas environment. Both young Frenchmen had facial and body tattoos and were accepted members of the Caddo tribe. They later testified that the Caddo were a gentle and kind people who wore large capes made of turkey feathers and dressed in antelope skins in cold weather.

The Hasinai welcomed de León and gave the soldiers food, but the Caddos also wanted horses. Even more important, they wanted guns and ammunition. They needed the weapons to defend themselves against the Osage tribe who lived to the northwest as well as their friends-turned-enemies, the Karankawas.

Massanet established two missions among the Caddo, but friendly relations did not last. The Spaniards refused to supply them with guns and ammunition. They abused and mistreated the Caddo women and tried to enslave the men. They did not respect the Caddo religion or the Caddo way of life. Perhaps even worse, they brought disease.

A year later, Domingo Terán de los Ríos led another expedition north from Mexico. They also searched for the French colony and found several French children with another band of the Karankawas. The children worked as slaves for their capturers. The Spanish traded a horse and some smoking tobacco for each of the French children.

On another expedition the priests heard about a "lady in blue." It was learned that the "lady in blue" was the Spanish Catholic Mother

María de Jesús de Ágreda, abbess of a Poor Clare's convent in Spain. While in a trance in Spain María "traveled" to Texas where she appeared and talked in the Caddoan language about Christianity. In 1620, she "came down from the hills" and spoke with members of the Hasinais group of Caddos. They called her "the lady in blue" because she wore a mantel (overdress) of blue. Later, she appeared to the Jumano of West Texas. The story of her visitations while in a trance was considered a myth, although several reports by early Spanish friars suggested that the bi-locations could be true.[7]

Over the decades of mission-building in Texas, the friars converted many native peoples from their own religious beliefs and rituals. Often, though, the native people just added the Christian God to their own spiritual beliefs.

THE TONKAWAS

The French settlers of La Salle's Fort St. Louis made contact with the Tonkawas in 1687, and regular European contact began by 1690 with the Spanish expedition of Alonso de León. Three Spanish missions using Indian labor were built for the Tonkawas between 1746 and 1769.

"Tonkawa" is a Waco Indian word meaning "they all stay together." The Tonkawas were a group of independent bands that probably migrated from the northern Plains tribes during the seventeenth century. They included various bands such as the Tonkawas proper, the Mayeyes, the Yerbipiames, and the Yojuanes, a Wichita band absorbed by the Tonkawas. They ranged between the middle and upper Brazos and Colorado Rivers. But Comanches and Apaches pushed them east and south into Central Texas near today's Austin and San Antonio.

The Tonkawa people seem to have been a "composite nation" made up of Indian people from numerous tribes speaking several languages and dialects all located in Central Texas. There were many, many "unattached" native people as a result of Apache raids, escape from the

A woodcut of the seventeenth-century "lady in blue." Institute of Texan Cultures illustration no. 68-2021

missions where they were used as slaves, people alone or in very small groups who survived the deadly, killer diseases, and small tribes relocating from other areas of the large territory. They all seemed to have come together as Tonkawas to fight their common enemy, the Apaches, and over the years developed a common culture. Clans within the

Tonkawas included bear, wolf, buffalo, snake, mouth open, blinking eyelids, and many others.[8]

After relocating to Central Texas, the Tonkawas prospered for a number of years, but not as farmers. The Tonkawas believed that before they were human, they had been wolves. As wolves hunted, so did the Tonkawas, or the Wolf People. The land had good hunting grounds that contained many buffalo and deer. They also hunted small game like rabbits, squirrels, raccoons, and even skunks. About the only game safe from the Tonkawa hunters were wolves and their coyote cousins.

As part of their religion, the Tonkawas worshiped wolves and other animals. They had a special ceremony honoring the wolves. The Tonkawas believed if the ceremony was done correctly nothing could harm them. They tattooed their faces and other body parts and wore earrings as ornaments for these important rites.

On the plains they made small conical huts of buffalo skin, but after relocating to Central Texas they adapted to using wood and brush huts for shelter. Men continued to hunt while Tonkawa women and girls gathered pecans, tunas of the prickly pear, eatable roots, fruit, acorns, and berries.

The men also fished in the rivers and streams. Sometimes the fishermen left fish in the open air. Insects gathered and laid eggs on the fish. The tribal members then ate the rotting fish and the insect larvae as a special treat.

A chief or subchief was chosen to rule each Tonkawa band, and a principal chief or head chief ruled the tribe. Women had great status. In fact, clans or bands claimed decent from women rather than men, forming a matrilineal culture. The Tonkawas also practiced a marital system that ensured care for widows and orphans. If a woman's husband died, she would marry her married sister's husband. Additionally, any children of the husband's children would inherit his property to keep it within the clan.

Like some other Texas tribes, the Tonkawas practiced ritual cannibalism that usually involved taking prisoners of war. The Tonkawas believed that by eating a bit of an enemy's flesh they acquired that person's courage and skills. After such rituals, warriors usually did a "scalp dance." Wearing war paint and their best clothes, the men formed a rotating circle around the women who held long poles with enemy scalps hanging from them. While they danced, the men made music with drums, reed whistles, and sticks and stones that were clapped together. The dancing extended well into the night.

The practice of cannibalism, beyond ritualistic and ceremonial, seems to have occurred among several Texas tribes, including the tribe Cabeza de Vaca and his men were with when they were stranded on Galveston Island. Some evidence suggests that the Atakapas, Karankawas, Caddos, and Tonkawas practiced cannibalism. Whether from starvation or as a regular practice, one account held that a Tonkawa band ate a captured Comanche. They cut him up and cooked him in a stew that included corn and other vegetables. After their big feast and rituals, the exhausted participants took a nap. But historians and archeologists are still debating this issue, and the above example of a Comanche being eaten may be another type of ritual cannibalism in which there was a spiritual transfer of strength from a warrior to his capturer.

The Wolf people were usually friendly to others except for the Comanches and Apaches, their historic enemies. The Comanches and Apaches raided the villages of the Tonkawas, stole goods, and took slaves.

Like some other Indians, the Tonkawas sometimes sought out the missions for protection. Some accepted the mission life of the Spanish priests, but the Tonkawas paid a high price for the protection. Catholic priests and soldiers used intimidation and violence to control them; treated them as inferiors; and used them to do all the work. The Spaniards took Indian women as desired, and the priests did not allow the Indians to perform their own rituals and ceremonies. Overall, the mission experience degraded and humiliated the native peoples. Many ran away and returned to their tribe while others remained and changed their ways.

The Comanche raiders eventually took over most of the Tonkawas land area, so in revenge the Tonkawas became scouts for the U.S.

▼▼▼

Army and the Texas Rangers, whose mission it was to defeat the Comanche. In 1859, the government sent the Tonkawas people to a reservation in Indian Territory. As late as 1905, reports stated that Tonkawas lived as farmers around Ponca City. The Tonkawas were still a recognized tribe and the town of Tonkawa, Oklahoma, had 3,299 people, some of whom were descendants of the Tonkawas.[9]

THE TIGUAS

The Tiguas are a Pueblo people who speak the Tewa language of their ancestors, who were from the New Mexico tribes at the Ysleta, Sandia, Taos, and Picuris Pueblos. Earlier Tigua ancestors lived at Gran Quivira in the Manzano Mountains southeast of today's Albuquerque. The building of Gran Quivira Pueblo started in A.D. 800. The people built additions to it every year, and by 1300 it was one of the largest pueblos in the southwest.

The Spanish explorer Vásquez de Coronado first made contact with the Pueblo Indians of New Mexico in the 1540s when the native people lived in thirteen villages. Three of the villages had more than two hundred dwellings. However, by 1680, their total population had decreased to about 2,000. New Mexico's Pueblo Indians had suffered for decades from enslavement by the Spaniards. After sustained deaths from diseases, drought, and famine, they revolted in 1680. Following this revolt about 315 of the Tiguas, fearing for their lives, fled from the enemy Indian tribes attacking, and left New Mexico and headed south with the fleeing Spaniards. A village called Ysleta del Sur (Isleta of the South) was created. The next year, the Spanish soldiers counterattacked New Mexico's pueblo of Ysleta, capturing some Tiguas. The soldiers forced the captives to join their kinsmen at Ysleta del Sur.

Meanwhile, the Tiguas helped establish the first permanent Spanish settlement in Texas. At today's El Paso the Spanish established two missions: Corpus Christi de la Ysleta and Nuestra Senora del Socorro. Coming from the village of Ysleta in New Mexico, the captured Tigua introduced the pueblo culture to West Texas, but because they were with the Spanish priests, most converted to Christianity while maintaining some of their native spiritual beliefs and rituals as well.

Upon arrival in Texas, the Tiguas had nothing. Wanting to recreate the life they left behind, they built pueblo buildings much like modern apartment buildings for housing. The buildings were two, three, or more stories high. Hundreds of families lived in the biggest ones that were subdivided into small apartments. Workers built them around a plaza where people gathered. Historically, all the families in a pueblo building were closely related. Living near family was important in the traditional way of life.

By 1750, approximately 500 Indians and some 54 Spaniards lived at Ysleta. By 1787, though, the Tiguas had entered a period of decline caused by diseases and numerous raids by the Plains Indians. The population shrunk to 195 people. In time, even their pueblos crumbled and they built *jacales*. A jacal was a small hut made of sticks stuck in the ground very close together and covered with mud. Each jacal had one front opening with no door.

The village Tiguas worked as farmers. The men dug irrigation ditches to bring in the water from the Rio Grande and cleared the fields where the women planted their crops of corn, beans, melons, and squash. Children worked with their mothers in the field. Women and girls continued to gather wild foods found in nature.

The men added to the diet by hunting wild game such as rabbits, deer, bear, and antelope. Women raised cotton and used it to make their clothes. Men raised sheep, and women made clothes of wool. The Tiguas also made pottery as they had in their northern villages of New Mexico.

The people depended on their crops and hunting to survive; therefore, many ceremonies occurred during the growing season. One dance occurred at the time for planting corn. Another came when "fresh" corn could be seen on the stalk. There were other dances for green corn, young corn, and mature corn. But the big-

A thatched roof jacal, c. 1913. Institute of Texan Cultures illustration no. 80-416

gest ceremony of all came at harvest time when they knew they had food to get through the winter. The corn dances generally took four days, and the people wore their finest traditional clothes. Celebrations included prayers, speeches by elders, music, ceremonial dances, games for all, and several feasts. Other rituals were geared to the hunt, in order to ensure the men had ample game and many kills.

Another Tigua ceremony from the Christian era is the Feast of St. Anthony, still held on June 13. Early on, St. Anthony became their patron saint. He protected them and their pueblos.

The early Tiguas missed their old pueblo homes and relatives left behind in New Mexico. They sang a sad song.

My home over there,
Now I remember it,
And when I see it,
The mountain far away
Oh, then I weep,
Oh, what can I do?[10]

A Tigua potter painting a piece prior to firing. Institute of Texan Cultures illustration no. 92-369, neg. 86-2-27ᵃ, courtesy of Bill Wright

As the Tigua desperately tried to survive in their new West Texas homes, French traders arrived in East Texas. In 1713, the French trader Louis Juchereau de Saint Denis and a party of traders and trappers from Louisiana appeared in the Caddo lands. Two survivors of the La Salle expedition, who had miraculously returned to France before coming again to the Louisiana area, led the traders. Both the French and Indians prospered from the new trade. Unlike the Span-

ish, Saint Denis traded guns and ammunition in return for Caddo goods. Moving farther south and trading as he traveled, Saint Denis reached a point near today's Eagle Pass on the Rio Grande in 1714. Spanish authorities arrested him and took him to Mexico City.

Saint Denis convinced the Spaniards of his intention to engage in peaceful trade. He returned to Texas with a Spanish expedition going back into Caddo country to establish more missions. At a site between the Trinity and Neches Rivers, the Spaniards built a *presidio,* or fort, and four missions. Using the Caddos as construction workers, the priests soon had many new missions in the area. The priests and friars hoped to Christianize the Caddos and the small bands of Coahuiltecans and Karankawas that still lived in the region.

In 1719, back in Europe, Spain and France went to war, and the fight affected the French and Spanish in East Texas. The French temporarily chased the Spaniards out of the area. But Spain soon recovered the lost ground. Meanwhile, the struggle of the two European powers had a major impact on the native peoples of Texas and their culture. Diseases continued to kill thousands in epidemics that spread across the land. The European presence disrupted the Indians' political, social, economic, and cultural life by trying to force the Indians to adopt European ways.

THE APACHES

All the native people in Texas wanted Spanish horses and French guns. Led by the Apaches who came first, the Plains Indians migrated south to be near the sources for the guns and horses. They incorporated other tribes reduced by war and disease, which expanded their ability to make raids on others. The major branches of Apaches included the Mescalero Apaches, Lipan Apaches, and Kiowa Apaches. The Comanches and Kiowas also moved south to expand their horse herds and acquire weapons. The arrival of all these tribes threatened other tribes, including the Jumanos. The Jumanos served as middlemen in a large trading network, which held annual trade fairs around La Junta. Buffalo hides were traded for Spanish horses, Caddo bows, and Pueblo textiles and turquoise. But the warlike Apache disrupted the trade pattern and caused the Jumanos to join the Spanish for survival.

The Jumanos tried to defeat the aggressive Apaches, but the raiders could not be conquered. Instead, Apaches almost exterminated the Jumanos. By the 1720s, the Jumanos had lost their unique identity as a tribe. Some survivors moved south into Mexico and eventually blended with the Indian population there. Others joined or married with their Apache enemy, which allowed them to survive.

The arrival of the Apaches spelled the end for other tribes. The word "Apache" (Apachu) was a Zuni word that means "enemy." Apaches called themselves Inde or Dine; both words mean "the people." Originating in Canada, they migrated south and eventually came into Texas. They arrived around 1530 and settled in villages where they farmed. They grew crops of corn, beans, and squash. They also ate the bulbs of the *sotol* and maguey, varieties of the agave plant. Women roasted the bulbs in rock-lined pits or ground the bulbs into flour. After the harvest, they moved with the hunting parties searching for the buffalo herds. In time, the buffalo became all-important to the Apaches, just as with other Plains tribes who followed the Apaches into Texas.

Hunting the buffalo on foot was difficult and dangerous work. A man could not outrun a buffalo, and the large animal might charge and gore a hunter to death. However, the Apaches hunted the animals anyway. Their favorite and safest way to make a "kill" was simply to stampede a herd or part of a herd over a cliff. Other Apaches at the foot of the cliff killed the injured animals with bows and arrows or they would stab the buffaloes with long spears.

Hunting changed when the Apaches got horses. They were the second native tribe to get horses; the Pueblo people of the New Mexico area were the first. With horses, the Apaches could ride into a buffalo herd, shooting arrows until several buffaloes fell. Then, the men finished their kill with knives or spears. If a buffalo charged, the hunter easily escaped on a swift horse. The Apaches also used

▼▼▼

A latter-day Apache known simply as Apache Jim, c. 1890. Institute of Texan Cultures illustration no. 89-129

A prime buffalo. Institute of Texan Cultures illustration no. 68-159

strong ropes that were woven from fibers of the *lechuguilla* plants that they used to drag the dead animals to a butchering area.

The Apaches maintained a social organization similar to other tribes: the extended family. Several related extended families formed a band. The most respected man in the band served as leader; with the advice of a council, he settled disputes.

The Apaches developed a good system of communication. They posted 24-hour-a-day guards and lookouts. Smoke signals and messengers warned the tribe of approaching enemies, buffalo stampedes, prairie fires, or other dangers.

As the Apaches moved farther into Texas, they continued attacking other Indian tribes, spreading terror. But the Apaches also had troubles. From the north came the equally powerful Comanches who arrived in West Texas about 1700. Although the horse allowed the Apaches to be nomadic and follow the buffalo herds, they continued their seasonal settlements, where they returned to their planted fields, looking forward to a new time of harvest. But when the Comanches found the settlements, they raided and killed the Apaches and destroyed their crops.

▼▼▼

A cowboy trades with two Plains Indians. Institute of Texan Cultures illustration no. 84-166

Apache oral tradition and documents record that an extended battle occurred in 1723 on the southern plains of West Texas. Plains Indians almost always fought guerrilla-style. They made lightning strikes and quickly rode away. But the 1723 fight was a stand-up, fight-to-the-end battle lasting nine days. The Apache made a final stand, but the Comanche won.

After the defeat, the Apache Nation split. The Mescalero Apaches moved into western Texas where the Jumanos once lived, and eventually moved farther west into New Mexico. The Lipan Apaches relocated to southeastern Texas and claimed the land between the Nueces River and the Rio Grande, once home to the Coahuiltecans and Karankawas. From there, they raided San Antonio and other settlements in the Rio Grande Valley. The Apache also took on the Tonkawas in Central Texas.[11]

THE COMANCHES

A Shoshone tribe, the Comanches had lived in villages and farmed west of the northern Rocky Mountains. But in the 1600s, they moved east across the mountains into eastern Wyoming. By 1680, the tribe had acquired horses from the Spaniards and the Pueblo Indians of New Mexico. They arrived in the West Texas plains by 1723 and moved into the Hill Country west of Austin by the 1740s. By 1750, the Comanches, along with their ally, the Kiowas, controlled an area of the southern plains called the Comanchería, or land of the Comanches. As "Lords of the South Plains" they controlled the area until the 1870s, over a period of more than one hundred years.

The Comanches only loosely could be called a tribe, as most lived and moved in smaller subgroups known as bands. The Comanches had twelve bands. The most important were the Penatekas, or honey eaters, and the Quahadies, or antelopes. It was the Penatekas band that first moved into Texas. Politically, the Comanches practiced democratic principles in their government. Each tribal band or subtribe had leaders chosen by the group, the most important being the civil chief. To maintain his leadership, the civil chief had to be fair and honest with his people, or he might lose his position. The warriors also chose their war chiefs, but the war chief's power might exist for only one campaign.

The Comanche owned three times more horses than any other tribe and controlled the breeding ground of the wild mustangs. Their primary concern was to increase the size of their horse herds.[12] Comanche warriors became experts in handling their horses. They were probably the second greatest light horsemen in world history. Only the horsemen of Mongolia who lived in the 1200s and 1300s might have been better. The Comanche Allen Mihecaby remembered the elders telling about their relationship with horses: "I think the Comanche Indians were known as the best horsemen in the world. . . . Wild herds of horses roamed the prairies and the Indians learned to capture and control them. . . . A Comanche Indian youth was taught to ride from childhood. . . . For this reason the Comanches . . . were frequently termed the 'Cossacks of the Plains.'"[13]

For the Comanche the buffalo was essential. They used almost every part of the animal for food, clothing, or shelter. A white Oklahoman recalled the care Comanche women took in tanning the buffalo hides:

> Tanning the animal hides by the Indians was of great importance as they used hides for so many different things. The Indians would take a new hide, let it dry a few days, then when it seemed to be dryed through[,] they would kill other animals and take the brains from them and rub them thoroughly on the underside after they had chiseled the hair off the other with a sharp, pointed rock. Working the brains over the hide was called curing it and this caused the hide to become soft. From this, moccasins were made. They also cut the soft side in narrow strips, using these for string.[14]

Boys were important in Comanche society. They needed to become great hunters to take care of their close and extended family. A father or uncle placed a male child on horseback when the boy was only a year or two old. With the boy tied securely to its back, the horse taught the boy to ride within a short time. Boys loved to shoot

Four Comanche men pose in a photography studio in 1890. Institute of Texan Cultures illustration no. 89-125

their bows and arrows. The boy who could shoot with accuracy and power earned a special status. Mihecaby recalled: "The little Indian boys of early days were taught to ride horses very young. They were told to ride behind an older man and kill a buffalo with a bow and arrow. They must learn the exact location of the heart of the buffalo, then they ride in a circle around the buffalo and the boy shoots it, then he is taught how to skin and prepare it to eat."[15]

Included in the teaching process was one of the Comanche ceremonies, the "eagle dance." During the dance, a warrior gave his son or nephew weapons and clothing decorated with the eagle's feathers. They believed that the boy gained strength and power from the feathers.

One white woman who lived among the Comanches commented about their care of babies: "One would never see an Indian baby out of his cradle board. This was something made of skins of animals, about two feet in length, made of round shape getting smaller at one end. The Indian baby is placed on his cradle board, laced in tightly, which makes the baby think he is being held close in his mother's arms. Then the cradle board is strapped on the Indian woman's back and she can go about doing her work."[16]

Unlike other Plains tribes the Comanches held few group ceremonies. They did not perform the Sun Dance, but worshiped the sun as a mediator. Their supreme God lived far away in the heavens. God lived so far away that He neither talked to the Comanches nor could they talk to Him. So the sun, closer to the Indians' Creator, became the "medium" that heard the Comanches' prayers and passed their words on to the great God.

The Comanches associated birth and life with breath. They believed that at the instant of death, most souls went directly to a place of the spirits. There were exceptions, such as a person who died in the dark or had been strangled or scalped. Rachael Plummer, a captive of the Comanches, found it odd that they mourned more for scalped warriors. She did not understand that scalping meant the warrior's spirit would never go to join other spirits. Meanwhile, relatives and friends went into deep mourning. The female relatives screamed, cried, tore at their clothing, and cut themselves with sharp knives. Males usually cut their hair short, a symbolic sign that they were in mourning.

The Comanches practiced both faith healing and the use of herbal plants to care for their sick. They used the purple coneflower or echinacea, which is today considered by some to be one of the world's most useful medicinal herbs. The Comanches used it as a remedy for toothaches and sore throats.

Medicine men performed various rituals for sick people from sunup to sundown, while others chanted to the sounds of shaken gourds and terrapin or turtle shells filled with pebbles. If a patient died then some error or improper attitude of the people in the ceremonies had occurred.

They have a strong belief in a Supreme Being; they are zealous in what they pretend to be; they believe it right to torture their prisoners and make slaves of them; they have a natural enmity against the white people; they believe in resurrection of the body. . . . The women are servants. I knew one young man [who had] his mother hung for refusing to get him some feathers to feather his arrows, and appeared to rejoice at her death. The women wait on the men—all the men do is kill the meat. The women butcher it, dress their skins, makes their mockosins [*sic*] and other clothing, herd their horses, saddles and pack and unsaddle and unpack them, build their camps, dress their meat, etc. The men dance every night, during which the women have to wait on them with water and other things . . . no woman is permitted in any of their councils. They often eat their meat entirely raw. There is a strong belief in Witchcraft.[17]

The Kiowas and their relatives the Kiowa Apaches became allied with the Comanches in Texas by 1750. The Kiowas once lived along the Yellowstone and Missouri Rivers in today's Montana. They were organized into six independent bands. Once they adapted to the horse, the need for more horses drew them southward. They also wanted the guns, slaves, and trade items available to the south.

Aggression characterized all the Plains tribes, and the men "counted coup" as a sign of a great warrior. The warriors were testing their skill to acquire status within the tribe. Coup could be acquired by unique acts of courage such as stealing (horses, for example) from an enemy camp or going into an enemy's tipi and touching him and/or his family without getting caught. Coup also could be gained by killing an enemy in hand-to-hand fighting during a raid or battle. Scalping was practiced, but they were little more than trophies. It is possible the Comanches only scalped enemies who were also known to take scalps. For coup to be counted, witnesses had to see it happen and testify about the deed to other warriors. Those with the most coups became judged as great warriors.

THE WICHITAS

The Wichitas lived in central Kansas in 1541 when Coronado's expedition passed through. He found them at the Great Bend of the Arkansas River where they lived in pit houses and farmed. Coronado recorded his impressions of the Quiviras [Wichitas]: "There are not more than twenty-five towns, with straw houses in it, nor any more in all the rest of the country that I have seen and heard about. . . . All they have is the tanned skins of the cattle [buffalo] they kill, for the herds are near where they live, at quite a large river. They eat meat raw like the Querechos [Apaches] and Tejas [Jumanos]. They are enemies of one another. . . . These people of Quivira [Wichitas] have the advantage over the others in their houses and in growing of maize [corn]."[18]

Raiding Osages living in present-day Missouri and Arkansas pushed the Wichitas southward. The Osages acquired European guns from the many Wichitas they killed. By 1719, the Wichitas had migrated into present-day Oklahoma where the French trader Jean Baptiste Bénand de La Harpe met them. By the 1750s, several bands of the Wichitas could be found living close to the riverbanks on both sides of the Red River. They were west-northwest of the East Texas Caddos, their kinsmen. Their settlements, called the Twin Villages, were located north of present-day Nocona, Texas, at Spanish Fort.

The Wichitas were active traders of long bows made of Bois de Arc wood, necklaces of elk teeth, tobacco, corn, and beans. Other tribes eagerly traded for the strong, flexible Bois de Arc bows. The Wichitas traded their surplus crops for Comanche horses and buffalo meat and hides. Then they traded some of the horses for French guns and ammunition and Caddo pottery.

▼▼▼

As kinsmen of the Caddos, the Wichitas practiced some of the Caddo ways. They farmed like their Caddo cousins, and they held extended harvest ceremonies. Even their dome-shaped housing resembled those of the Caddos.

Most Wichita lodges were large, from fifteen to thirty feet wide. Each lodge had from ten to fifteen pallets for an extended family. When it became too crowded, a family or two built a new lodge close by. Near their lodges, the Wichitas also built arbors for shade during the hot months. They made the arbors by pounding four poles into the ground and by placing other poles side-by-side for a roof. Then, dried grass and wood debris covered the poles to complete the roof. In the shade of the arbors, protected from the sun, women made clothes, dried buffalo hides and meat, dried pumpkins and corn, and cooked.

In addition to fields of maize or corn, the Wichitas also planted great fields of pumpkins, beans, and squash. They grew watermelons, muskmelons, and also planted plum trees. The tribe temporarily moved west for the annual buffalo hunts and then returned.

Many Wichita celebrations—like those of other Indians—showed their concern about having enough food, especially corn, to survive the harsh cold months. All through the seasonal cycle of growing corn, the people had prayers and gatherings. They wore beautiful clothing and participated in ceremonial dances and feasts.

Women wore clothes made of tanned hides. They dressed to cover their bodies from chin to ankles and wore treasured necklaces of elk teeth. Men wore shirts and loincloths covered by leggings. The Wichitas tattooed themselves around their eyes. The tattoos made their eyes resemble raccoon eyes. They even called themselves Kitikiti'sh, which means raccoon eyes. Compared to various other tribes, the Wichitas were shorter, stockier, and darker.

The Wichita bands included the Wichita proper, the Tawakonis, the Taovayas, the Iscanis, and the Toweashes. Law and order among the Wichitas involved a principal chief and subchiefs from different clans. But before taking any actions, the chief and subchiefs sought the advice of the adult male tribal members.

When problems arose, warriors attended a council where they smoked the peace pipe. They did this to show they intended to be reasonable and would try to make a good decision. When not in use, the pipe was kept in the lodge of the clan's chief. Should adults commit wrongs, their extended relatives threatened to avoid them and refused to help them unless the wrongdoers assumed an attitude of humbleness and stopped committing bad acts.

The Wichita's religious leaders were known as shamans. They did not worship the sun. They were stargazers, which meant they worshiped the stars.[19]

In 1758 the Wichitas temporarily united with the Comanches, Caddos, and Tonkawas against the Spanish and the raiding Lipan Apaches. A large force of two thousand warriors with French guns appeared at San Sabá mission. The combined tribal nations killed approximately forty Lipans and Spaniards. The raiders looted and burned the mission. The Spanish soldiers in the nearby presidio feared for their lives, offered little help, and remained in their fort throughout the battle.

In 1759, Col. Diego Ortiz Parrilla, commander of the San Sabá presidio, assembled six hundred men, mostly Spaniards, with some

A traditional Wichita village in the 1890s. Institute of Texan Cultures illustration no. 89-140

Wichita Religious Beliefs

▼▼▼

The Wichitas believed in many gods and goddesses. They called their supreme God "Not-Known-to-Man," Kinnikasus. For the Wichitas, God's ways, power, and knowledge could never be fully understood by mankind. Kinnikasus created the world and all that was in it. Wichitas included him in their prayers and religious ceremonies.

Lesser gods included a Sun God or Man-Reflecting-Light; the spirit of the first man on earth, or Morning Star, who was associated with daylight; the South Star, or guardian of all the warriors; the Wind God, whose breath brought babies to life; and the North Star, or The-Light-that-Stands-Still, who gave men a sense of direction. They feared the North Star because he brought death.

Lipans. He directed his army northward until he reached the Wichita Twin Villages on the Red River. The Taovaya band had built an impressive fort with four underground rooms to hide their women and children during battle.

Parrilla's forces reached "Spanish Fort," as it was later misnamed, and saw a French flag flying over it. Inside were Frenchmen, Taovayas, other Wichitas, and Comanches ready to fight. After a four-hour battle, the Spanish force retreated in defeat. Following Parrilla's disaster, Spanish power over the native people of Texas virtually collapsed, and at no time did Spanish power extend north beyond the Red River.[20]

The Comanches, Lipan Apaches, and Mescalero Apaches continued their raids over the years, acquiring control over much of the future state of Texas. They viewed the prosperous Spanish settlements as good sources of plunder for stealing horses, cattle, sheep, weapons, ammunitions, and other supplies. They attacked wagon trains and raided the Tonkawas and Tawakonis in Central and East Texas.

Meanwhile Spain had its own problems with other parts of its colony of New Spain (Mexico). In 1810 Father Miguel Hidalgo and his followers in the town of Dolores, Guanajuato, declared for freedom. Although Hidalgo's early movement failed, others took up the cause. Mexico won its independence from Spain after the struggles of 1820–1821.

THE AMERICAN INVASION

Americans had entered Texas as early as the 1790s when Philip Nolan arrived trading for horses to pay his debts. In 1800, he led an American group of private citizens who stormed into Texas and tried to take it from Spain. The Spaniards caught and executed him.

In 1813, the Mexican revolutionary José Bernardo Gutiérrez de Lara began another attempt to wrest Texas from Spain. He joined forces with Augustus Magee, an American, and gained control of Nacogdoches, Goliad, and San Antonio. However, Spanish forces

▼▼▼

defeated them at the Battle of Medina. In 1819, Dr. James Long of Natchez, Mississippi, led yet another armed invasion into Texas. His forces captured Nacogdoches, but Spaniards later captured him. The Spaniards put Dr. Long in prison where one of the prison guards killed him. These efforts by Americans caused problems for the Caddos of East Texas who chose to remain peaceful and neutral.[21]

After Mexico gained independence and worked to set up a government, American pioneers from the east arrived in Texas. These descendants of Europeans, who had settled along the Atlantic Coast and fought their own war of independence against the British Empire in 1775, came seeking land and prosperity in the west. The Americans brought more life-threatening change to all the native people of Texas. The genocide soon to be waged by settlers and later government policy further destroyed the native people and their culture.

The Americans from the southern states with their slaves were moving into Texas by the 1820s and were pushing the Indian tribes westward. Cherokee, Chickasaw, Choctaw, Alabama-Coushatta, and Creek began moving into Texas. Especially numerous were the Cherokees. Most of the arriving tribes were farmers and stock-raisers like the Caddo.

Hundreds of Cherokee followed Chief Duwali (Bowl) in 1810 as he moved his people from western North Carolina into Missouri, then into Arkansas, and in 1819 into East Texas north of Nacogdoches. Generally, the Caddo welcomed the native migrants who were distantly related as helpful allies in their fights against the raiding Comanche, Apache, and Osage. After Mexico achieved independence from Spain, Mexican authorities welcomed the new tribes, hoping they would act as a buffer and defense against the Euro-Americans coming into their territory. Mexican leaders even promised land titles to the Indians, promises they did not keep.

As the 1820s became the 1830s, Americans continued to enter Texas in larger numbers. Still, the Plains tribes like the Comanches went on raiding, only now they attacked isolated farmsteads and small villages of whites. Yet Euro-Americans poured into the re-

Goddesses included Bright-Shining-Woman, or the Moon Goddess, the first woman that Kinnikasus created. As the wife of Morning Star, the Wichitas believed her to be the mother of the universe. Most important to women, the Moon Goddess controlled reproduction in the natural, animal, and human world. Woman-having-powers-in-the-Water, or the Water Goddess, brought the cleansing aspect of water and its healing properties, too. Another important goddess was Earth Mother.

The Wichitas held frequent ceremonies to honor the gods and goddesses and to gain their favor.

Cherokee Foods

▼▼▼

Cherokee people, once inhabitants of East Texas, ate simple, hearty foods. They seasoned their meats with salt, and the women cooked the meat in clay pots. Women prepared corn by boiling or roasting it over an open fire. By grinding the corn kernels between stones, a coarse meal resulted. Sometimes they also ground nuts and seeds, like sunflower seeds, and mixed them into the cornmeal. Then they added water and salt and shaped the dough into cornbread. They baked the mixture in an outdoor earthen-oven similar to a Pueblo horno.

They also made tsu-ya-ga, a bean bread in which beans and corn were boiled separately. When the beans became soft, the women poured some of

gion, and before long they outnumbered the Mexicans and the Indian people of Texas.

Problems existed between Mexico and the white Americans from the start. The differences led the Texas settlers to revolt in 1835–36, but the Indians of East Texas posed a potential danger to them. If a great number of them sided with Mexico, the Texans would fail to achieve independence.

General Sam Houston, commander of the rebel army, realized the importance of the Indians to the Texan cause. He met with some of their leaders, convinced them to remain neutral, and made treaties with a number of the tribes. The tribes included bands of Cherokee, Alabama-Coushatta, Delaware, Kickapoo, Shawnee, Biloxi, Quapaw, Choctaw, and remnants of the Caddo tribes. Houston promised them a large reservation in East Texas. There, they could live their traditional lifestyles and continue their culture. They could use their own laws to govern as long as those laws did not conflict with Texas laws.

With these treaties, the East Texas Indians thought they had achieved security and could live on their own land. However, the Republic of Texas government later refused to honor Houston's treaties.

After Texas gained independence from Mexico and set up the Republic, troubles erupted between the Mexican settlers who had lived in Texas for generations, called Tejanos, and the new settlers coming from the United States. The American and European settlers took Mexican lands and gave them to American pioneers who also displaced Mexicans as government officials. Some Mexicans became angry and rebelled. Led by Vicente Córdova, Mexicans and Tejanos started raiding white farms and settlements. Some Indians also fought with Córdova. In one attack near today's Tyler, raiders killed at least eighteen members of the Killough family.

Texas' political leader, President Mirabeau Lamar, hated Indians. He blamed the Cherokees and their associated tribes for killing the Killough family. Now, Lamar, using the Texas army, had an excuse to attack both Córdova and the native people.

▼▼▼

the bean broth into the cornmeal and mixed it. Then they added the beans and corn to the dough. They dropped small balls of the dough into boiling water to cook. Bean bread is similar to dumplings.

But their favorite was se-lu a-su-li tu-ya, a thick soup made of hominy and beans. The women mixed cooked beans with the hominy made from kernels of corn. As they cooked the beans and hominy, they added strips of pumpkin. When the pumpkin strips were soft, the cooks added cornmeal, ground walnuts, and ground hickory nuts. Then they added just enough molasses to sweeten the dish.

A drawing of Cherokee Chief Bowl by William A. Berry. Institute of Texan Cultures illustration no. 68-59

Chief Placido of the Tonkawa. Institute of Texan Cultures illustration no. 70-17

In 1839, a two-day Battle of the Neches began with Tonkawa Chief Placido and some forty of his warriors joining the Texans. They served as scouts, found the Cherokees, and joined the Texan attack. Aided by the Tonkawas, the Texans defeated the Cherokees and their associated tribes. They killed the great Cherokee leader, Chief Bowl, during the battle. Afterwards, to survive, most of the remaining Cherokee people escaped into Indian Territory or went south, hoping to get to Mexico.[22]

The Alabama and the Coushatta differed from some of the other tribes. These Muskegon tribes had once been members of the Upper Creek Confederation in the southeastern woodlands. As closely related tribes, the Alabama and Coushatta were often considered a single tribe. Their culture was much like the old Caddos and the later Cherokees. They actively supported the Texas Revolution, and the revolutionaries were grateful. They never resisted the government of the Republic of Texas. They never struck back when harmed. The Republic of Texas gave them a reservation on the lower Trinity River where they remain today, although in a greatly reduced land area.

With Indian matters in East Texas settling down, the leaders of the Republic looked to West Texas. There, the Comanches and their ally, the Kiowas, presented a major worry. The Comanches continued to raid isolated farms and small settlements. In the summer of 1836, Comanches took more than one hundred horses from pioneers who lived on the West Texas frontier.

The Comanches hated the settlers, even more than their Indian enemies. From the beginning, misunderstandings between the Texans and Comanches had occurred. A major misunderstanding included "gift exchanges." Gift exchanges represented a cultural cornerstone not only among the Comanches and Kiowas, but also to all Indian tribes.

From the Indian perspective, gift giving turned strangers into kinsmen, turned potential enemies into friends. The gift exchange created a special bond between people and created mutual obligations. Among the obligations was a rule: once the exchange took place, the negotiators would not fight or harm each other during the meeting or visit. No meeting, no negotiation, no council could begin without an exchange of gifts.[23]

Americans never understood the ritual of gift giving. They viewed the gifts as a bribe or as extortion, giving only because they felt a threat. Usually, Americans refused to participate in the ceremony, which insulted the native people. The Indians viewed American refusals as grounds for war and sometimes, an immediate battle followed.

The practice of "blood revenge" also led to violence. "Blood revenge" occurred whenever an enemy killed anyone in another warriors' clan or band. Thus, when a group killed Indians, the Indians struck back. But, the Indians out for revenge frequently did not distinguish among those individuals who were guilty or those who were not guilty. If Americans killed one of their own, they attacked the first American group that they came across. The settlers then branded the warriors as pure savages who must be exterminated. Then the Americans would seek revenge.

The settlers would organize a militia or send for the army and would kill the first Indians they encountered without bothering to find out if the Indians they fought were guilty or innocent of the original attack. A cycle of violence ensued.

Anglo leaders never grasped the fact that most tribes, especially the Plains Indians, organized themselves as clans or bands, each with its own chief. The action or treaties of one chief did not bind any other tribal group. Yet the whites viewed the entire Comanche Nation as guilty if any band under a single chief committed an outrage.

THE LIPAN APACHES

The Lipan Apaches, bitter enemies of the Comanches, made a proposal to the Texas government in the late 1830s. The Lipan Apaches wanted soldiers to join them in a joint expedition against the Comanche. Texas leaders agreed to the plan.

Mow-way (Shaking Hand), Yamparika chief and later chief of Quadhada Comanche, c. 1875. Institute of Texan Cultures illustration no. 68-158

In February of 1839, the Texans and Lipan Apaches located a Comanche village in the San Sabá Valley. Taking the Comanches by surprise, they killed or wounded many warriors, women, and children. The Comanche band regrouped and fought off their attackers and forced the Texans and Lipan Apaches to retreat. As they moved back, the Texans and Lipan Apaches soon confronted numerous other Comanche bands arriving to save their kin. The Comanches defeated the Texans and Lipan Apaches and took all their horses. The defeated attackers with their wounded walked a hundred miles back to their settlements.

▼▼▼

Then the Texas Rangers set out in pursuit of the Comanches. When the Rangers found the Comanche villages, they killed all the men, women, and children they could find and destroyed all food supplies. They took or killed the horses before burning the villages. From the north, the Cheyennes and Arapahoes also raided the Comanches. The numerous attacks greatly weakened the Comanches. More deaths occurred from several smallpox epidemics among the Comanche bands.

To end the killings, the Comanches wanted to make peace. Their peacemakers arrived in San Antonio in January, 1840. In negotiations, the Texas representatives made several demands. First, the

A drawing of an attack on an Indian village by the U.S. Cavalry in 1887. Institute of Texan Cultures illustration no. 70-586

Texans wanted the Comanches to return all white captives. Next, the Comanches must abandon Central Texas and cease attacking the settlements.

Comanches responded to the demands on March 19. Thirty-three Penateka Comanche leaders and warriors came to the Council House in San Antonio. The Indian leaders were ready to negotiate in order to stop the Ranger attacks. The Texans had demanded the Comanches release their white captives, but they brought only a few Mexican children and Matilda Lockhart, a 16-year-old girl they had captured.

Matilda told Texas officials the Comanches had fifteen other captives that the Indians intended to ransom one at a time. The leader, Muk-wah-ruh, said that other unrepresented Comanche bands held the other captives. The Texas leaders did not understand that the Comanches did not function as a totally united group and that the chiefs could not make decisions for the other bands.

A painting by Lee Herring of the Comanche chiefs arriving in San Antonio with captive Matilda Lockhart. Institute of Texan Cultures illustration no. 95-337

▼▼▼

79

Comanche Chief Buffalo Hump

▼▼▼

The Comanches came to the Council House in San Antonio to negotiate a peace treaty in 1840. They came under a white flag of truce. At the meeting the Texans made demands the Comanche band could not meet. The Texans pulled out guns and threatened to kill the Comanches if the demands were not met. When the fight started the Comanche ambassadors and chiefs used knives against solders armed with rifles. The Texans killed many Comanches.

After the Council House massacre of Comanche chiefs, the Penateka Comanches vowed revenge. With many chiefs dead, they united under Comanche War Chief Buffalo Hump.

Buffalo Hump raided down the

Not understanding Comanche ways, the Texans tried to take the Comanche leaders hostage until more captives were freed. A fight broke out in the Council House where the Comanches, armed only with knives, stabbed several soldiers. The Texans killed all twelve chiefs in the Council House. The warriors outside began to fight.

Comanche Chief Buffalo Hump. Institute of Texan Cultures illustration no. 68-153

▼▼▼

An 1871 cartoon by Thomas Nast telling an Indian to get out of the way of white settlers. Institute of Texan Cultures illustration no. 73-1545

When the fight ended, the Texans had killed thirty-five Comanches and imprisoned twenty-seven more, including some women and children. The Indians lost one hundred horses and many buffalo hides brought for the gift exchange.[24]

The massacre of Comanche chiefs and others who came in peace to the Council House refueled the Comanche hatred. Peace ambassadors should not be victims of violence. In their anger, the various Comanche bands tortured and killed some of the remaining captives. They assembled 1,000 men with Chief Buffalo Hump as their leader and raided deep into Texas, not stopping until they reached the Gulf Coast. They attacked and looted Victoria and moved on to virtually destroy the port-city of Linnville.

A volunteer army of Texans from the Colorado River counties cut off the Comanches' path home to the west. Texas Rangers joined the volunteer army as well as Chief Placido and about a dozen of his Tonkawa warrior-scouts. On August 11, 1840, the Texans beat the Comanches at the Battle of Plum Creek, and the volunteer army began to push the Comanches westward.[25]

Guadalupe Valley across southeastern Texas. For years, Buffalo Hump resisted the taking of Comanche lands. Finally, in defeat, Chief Buffalo Hump signed the Treaty of Council Springs, in which the Comanche lost much of their land and promised to remain at peace forevermore.

In 1856, he led his people to the new Brazos Indian Reservation. Once there, horse thieves preyed upon the Comanche. Farmers invaded the reservation and took the land. Two years later, Buffalo Hump led his people to Indian Territory where he signed a new treaty with military authorities at Camp Arbuckle. The Comanches set up their main camp in the Wichita Mountains. Unaware of Buffalo Hump's new treaty, Maj. Earl Van Dorn and his troops attacked the camp.

After the slaughter of more of his people, the chief led those remaining to the Comanche-Kiowa reservation where they gave up their traditional Comanche way of life.

A Comanche camp, c. 1854. Institute of Texan Cultures illustration no. 68-77

When Texas became part of the United States in 1845 the relationship between the Texans and the native peoples changed. Now Texas was a part of a much bigger and stronger political and military body. The federal government authorized the U.S. Army to build a string of forts across Texas to protect settlers from Indian attacks. The forts ran from today's Fort Worth to Eagle Pass, cutting through much of Central Texas.

In the 1850s, as settlers pushed farther into West Texas, the government responded by having the army build more forts to protect them as well as establish mail routes to El Paso. Also during the 1850s federal officials changed the Indian policy from extermination and killing of the native people to confinement on small reservations in undesirable locations or places that the pioneers did not want to settle. The goal was to confine the native people to specific areas and make the west safe for settlers. Texas agreed with the new policy and set aside 53,136 acres for two reservations. The Comanches would locate on land on the upper Clear Fork of the Brazos River. The Tawakonis, Wacos, and Tonkawas would locate near today's Graham.

The policy did not work. Most Comanches refused to settle in the area assigned to them. They frequently left the reservation to continue their old way of life hunting buffaloes. The old ways also included raiding white settlements, farms, and ranches.[26]

When the American Civil War began in 1861, the new Confederate government needed men to serve in the war. When the soldiers left the frontier, the raids by the native people increased once again. The Comanches and their Kiowa allies continued to escape government control.

The Comanches and Kiowas raided wagon trains on the Santa Fe Trail. General James H. Carleton ordered Col. Christopher "Kit" Carson to lead a winter expedition against the warrior tribes. After finding the camp of Kiowa-Apache Chief Dohasan, Carson and his men attacked and inflicted a mighty defeat on the Kiowas. After the battle, Carson directed his men to the old fort ruins at Adobe Walls, not knowing about a nearby five-hundred-tipi camp of Comanche.

Plains Indians on horseback, c. 1890. Institute of Texan Cultures illustration no. 84-189

More bands arrived until the Comanche numbered around seven thousand. Soon a battle raged with attacks and counterattacks. The whites eventually got the better of the Indians and killed the Kiowa-Apache Chief Iron Shirt. The power of the Comanches and Kiowas, though, was not broken, but Carson and his forces had won a major victory.

In 1867, some Plains tribes signed the Treaty of Medicine Lodge Creek. They accepted reservations in present-day Oklahoma. But the treaty had the same weakness of other Indian treaties. Not all chiefs and warriors accepted the terms. Chiefs who did accept the terms could speak only for their band or tribe.[27]

Nevertheless, the 1867 talks among the federal government and Indian leaders had great meaning. Comanche Chief Ten Bears spoke, and Sen. John B. Henderson spelled out the differences between the whites and the native people. Ten Bears heard that the peace commissioners intended to put his people on a reservation and teach them how to farm. The Americans also would build the Indians houses and churches. Then, the famous chief rose to give his statement. He said:

> I do not want the churches and the houses. I was born upon the prairie where the wind blew free and there was nothing to break the light of the sun. . . . I want to die there and not within walls. I know every stream and every wood between the Rio Grande and the Arkansas. I have hunted and lived over that country. I live like my fathers before me and like them I live happily. . . . When I was in Washington the Great Father told me that all the Comanche land was ours and that no one should hinder us from living upon it . . . we only wish to wander over the prairie until we die.

Senator Henderson responded to Ten Bears, saying:

> The buffalo will not last forever . . . [they] are now becoming few . . . the Indian must change the road his father trod, or he must suffer, and probably die . . . the whites are settling up all the good lands.

▼▼▼

They have come to the Arkansas River. When they come they drive out the buffalo. If you oppose them, war must come. They are many and you are few. You may kill some of them, but others will come and take their places. And finally, many of the Red Men will have been killed. . . . Now, before all the good lands are taken by whites, we wish to set aside a part of them for [you] . . . we propose to make that home on the Red River around the Wichita Mountains.[28]

Henderson's predictions of the future proved true.

CHAPTER 3

The Continuing Struggle to Survive

AFTER THE VARIOUS TRIBAL BANDS signed the Treaty of Medicine Lodge, President U. S. Grant pursued a "peace policy." He hoped to educate and "civilize" the Plains Indians by turning them into peaceful farmers. He hoped that they would just blend into American life. The policy failed.

The Plains Indians had no desire for the American version of education. They had no intention of becoming farmers. Most simply wanted to return to their old lifestyle. They lived to chase the buffalo. They wanted to live in freedom, moving from place to place, not be trapped on a reservation.

Many of the native people may have been like the fierce Kiowa warrior Satank (Sitting Bear). Born in 1800 in present-day Kansas, he became a warrior. A muscular man, he stood about five-foot ten-inches tall. When fighting, his movements were very quick and quiet. He eventually became a member of the Koitsenkos, the elite Kiowa warrior society.

In the Indian wars, Satank first fought the Cheyennes. Then he led Kiowa warriors in the fight against the Sac and Fox tribe. He attacked white settlements, wagon trains, and army outposts. In 1864, he led a raid on the settlers at Menardville on the San Saba River. He and his warriors killed many whites. Later, Satank seemed to change. As one of the Kiowas who had signed the treaty that removed his tribe to Indian Territory, he accompanied thousands of other Indian groups into today's Oklahoma. But, once there, he never accepted reservation life. He frequently left the reservation

An 1869 engraving from Harper's Weekly *illustrating America's idea of education for the Indian people.* Institute of Texan Cultures illustration no. 73-1488

and returned to the life of a nomad and continued leading raids. In 1870, he learned a white man had killed and scalped his son, also named Satank. Now the old warrior's hatred for whites knew no bounds.

Satank joined Kiowa Chief Satanta (White Bear) and a young warrior named Addo-etta (Big Tree). The three leaders recruited Kiowas, Comanches, Apaches, Arapahos, and Cheyennes. More than one hundred Indians left their reservations. They crossed the Red River and slipped into West Texas on May 15, 1870.

On May 18 the warriors raided a wagon train on the road between Fort Griffin and Fort Richardson. This raid became known as the Battle of Salt Creek. They killed seven members of the wagon train. Five of the teamsters managed to escape. After the attack, Satank and the other warriors returned to their reservations.

When the Salt Creek killings occurred, Gen. William Tecumseh Sherman was touring western Texas. As general of all the U.S. Armies, he wanted to learn first-hand about frontier conditions. Sherman thought that the Texans exaggerated the threat posed by the Indians, but he soon changed his mind.

At Fort Richardson, General Sherman learned of the Salt Creek killings from the teamster survivors. The tale shocked Sherman. Earlier, he and his men had been on the same road where the attack took place. In fact, Satank and the other warriors allowed Sherman's military train to pass as they waited for an easier target. Sherman now decided that the Indians should be removed from the frontier of Texas. He obtained permission to begin a campaign against all Indian people who refused to live on the reservations. Sherman traveled on to Fort Sill where he encountered Satank who had come to get rations. Satank openly bragged about the attack

Cheyenne, Comanche, and Kiowa captured and taken to prison at Ft. Marion, Florida, c. 1876. Several were arrested near the Red River. Institute of Texan Cultures illustration no. 68-1438

and of Satanta and Addo-etta joining him in the raid on the wagon train.

Sherman arrested the three warriors. A military guard hand-cuffed all three and placed chains around their ankles. Soldiers then loaded them onto a wagon to take them back to Fort Richardson to be put on trial for murder. While still near Fort Sill, Satank at-

Kiowa Chief Satanta.
Institute of Texan Cultures
illustration no. 68-85

▼▼▼

90

Kiowa Chief Addo-etta.
Institute of Texan Cultures
illustration no. 68-91

tempted an escape. Under a blanket, he managed to free himself from the handcuffs. Waving a knife that he had hidden in his clothing, he grabbed a guard's rifle and knocked him out of the wagon, but Satank never fired the rifle. Other guards shot and wounded him. They then pitched him out of the wagon and left him on the ground where he bled to death. Later, Tonkawa military scouts scalped him.

Meanwhile, the army's campaign against the Indians continued. Sherman needed someone to lead the army, and he chose the young cavalry officer Col. Ranald MacKenzie. He commanded the Fourth Cavalry Regiment, stationed at Fort Concho, near San Angelo. His regiment chased and fought the native people of Texas off and on from 1871 to 1875.[1]

THE BLACK SEMINOLES

In his campaign Mackenzie enlisted the help of the Black Seminoles living in Mexico. Before the Civil War, runaway slaves regularly escaped to Florida and encountered the Seminole Indians. The Seminoles offered protection to the black men and women who then paid tribute or taxes to them. Over the years men and women from the villages intermarried, which gave rise to what became known as the Black Seminole tribe.

As part of the forced migration to Oklahoma the Seminoles and Black Seminoles joined the Five Civilized Tribes. But when they ar-

Fort Sill, where the army supervised the Indians of the southern plains. Institute of Texan Cultures illustration no. 89-147

Black Seminole scouts.
Institute of Texan Cultures
illustration no. 68-1098

rived in Indian Territory, relations between the other tribes and the Black Seminoles were not good. Fearing enslavement by the new tribes living in Indian Territory, some of the Black Seminoles left for Mexico with Chief Wild Cat. The Mexican government gave the newcomers a land grant in Mexico. The Mexicans hoped the presence of the Black Seminoles would stop the Comanches and Apaches from raiding their settlements in northern Mexico.

In August of 1870, U.S. Army leaders met with Black Seminole leader John Kibbetts and requested scouts who could help stop the raids. Kibbetts agreed to help and several Black Seminole families moved to Fort Duncan in Texas. Kibbetts became a sergeant in the army while ten of his men served as privates. By the end of 1871, the army had hired twenty more Black Seminoles for scout duty against attacking Indians.

The Black Seminole scouts were experienced horsemen and marksmen. Some of them spoke several native languages. They helped the army negotiate with the different tribes and served with distinction along the Texas border with Mexico. Other scouts joined Colonel MacKenzie to help in his campaign against the Comanches and Kiowas.[2]

In addition to the white settlers and soldiers, the Plains Indians now faced competition from commercial buffalo hunters. The buffalo

William Dixon, Buffalo Hunter

William "Billy" Dixon came west from West Virginia. After holding a variety of jobs, he became a buffalo hunter. An excellent marksman, he earned a lot of money. When he went hunting, he could keep ten buffalo skinners busy all day, every day.

By 1874, he hunted in the Texas Panhandle. From a kill site, he hauled his hides by the wagonloads and stored them at Adobe Walls.

The Plains Indians hated the buffalo hunters because they only took the hides. Hunters like Billy eventually killed millions of the buffaloes, which the Comanches and Kiowas needed. Without the animals, the traditional way of life would end for the Plains tribes. The Indians began attacking the hunters.

On June 27, 1874, seven hundred Indians

A buffalo hunter's camp in the Texas Panhandle in 1874. Institute of Texan Cultures illustration no. 68-96

hunters wanted only the hides. A new method for tanning the hides had been developed and people in the eastern United States and Europe wanted good tanned leather goods. The demand pushed the price of hides up to around three dollars apiece, a price that attracted many professional hunters.

Englishman Walter J. Collinson came to America at sixteen, and by 1874, he was in Texas. He became a partner with Jim White and Thomas L. Causey, buffalo hunters who ran a six-mule, two-wagon outfit. After buying supplies at Fort Griffin, Collinson headed west. He stopped when he reached the Llano Estacado and began killing buffaloes. After one trip in the spring of 1877, he returned to Fort Griffin with 11,000 hides, 45,000 pounds of dried meat, and 6,000 tongues.

The Texas Legislature considered trying to save the animals from extinction, but Gen. Philip Sheridan protested. Sheridan claimed that if hunters continued to slaughter the buffaloes, the Plains tribes would lose their major food source. Then they would be forced to accept peace and remain on their reservations. Texas leaders agreed with Sheridan and took no action against the buffalo hunters. The killing continued, and by 1880, only a few hundred buffaloes were left.

The killing of the buffalo made the Plains Indians angrier. The Comanche and Kiowa started attacking the camps of the hunters in addition to the homes of settlers on the frontier. In June, 1874, the Indians formed a war party with about seven hundred Comanche, Kiowa, and Cheyenne warriors. They attacked twenty-eight buffalo hunters at Adobe Walls in the Panhandle near the town of Borger.[3] Herman Asanap's father fought with the Indians at Adobe Walls and told Herman about it. "Father was a friend and warring partner of Chief Quanah Parker; he was in the battle of Adobe Walls. . . . The Comanches were a very wild tribe and hard to subdue. They hated the white man because they [sic] killed all the buffalo . . . they made a vow to fight the whites and kill as many as possible. . . . The battle [of Adobe Walls] kept up several days and only two white men were killed but over one hundred Indians were killed or wounded. Quanah Parker was wounded in the back of the head."[4]

Humiliated in their defeat, the Indians increased their raids on the settlers. In 1875, Colonel MacKenzie set out with his Black Seminole scouts and a group of six hundred troopers to find the warriors. The Black Seminole scouts found the Indians' camps in Palo Duro Canyon in West Texas. MacKenzie then launched attacks on five separate Comanche villages.

During this battle, Black Seminole scout Adam Payne fought with great courage. Later, he received the U.S. Medal of Honor. Many Indians escaped, but the troopers destroyed their camps, burned their dwellings, took all the food, and killed more than one thousand horses.

attacked at Adobe Walls. Quanah Parker led the assault party.

Billy Dixon, along with twenty-seven other men and one woman, ran into the saloon and stores to defend themselves. The Indians surrounded the town. The siege lasted for several days, but on the second day Billy Dixon became famous.

A group of Cheyenne appeared on a mesa, overlooking the encampment. Dixon shot one of the Indians off his horse. The Indian was seven-eighths of a mile away!

After the battle, Dixon became a U.S. Army scout for several years and received the Medal of Honor for heroic actions. He returned to civilian life in 1883 to work as a cowboy on a ranch near Adobe Walls. He died on March 9, 1913.

▼▼▼

Without food or horses, the Indians faced starvation. They had no choice but to return to the reservation. By June, 1875, even the gallant and brave Comanche Chief Quanah Parker surrendered. He now believed that the Indians must change or they would surely die. Parker led his people to adopt white ways. He began to use his white mother's maiden name, Parker. He remained the principal chief of the Comanche and continued to "take the white man's road."[5]

Even after Parker surrendered with his band, other tribes continued their raids, attacking along the border between Texas and Mexico. On April 14, 1878, a band of forty Kickapoos, Lipan Apaches, Seminoles, Mexicans, and a white man, wearing war paint, raided Duval and Nueces Counties.

Comanche Chief Quanah Parker, c. 1889. Institute of Texan Cultures illustration no. 68-144

Fay July (left) *and William Shields* (right), *who served as Black Seminole scouts.*
Institute of Texan Cultures illustration no. 68-1011

Prairie Flower

The Quadhada band of the Comanche raided Fort Parker in 1835 and captured nine-year-old Cynthia Ann Parker. She grew up among the Comanche and accepted their way of life. As a young woman, she married Quadhada Comanche Chief Peta Nocona. She had a son, Quanah, and a daughter, Prairie Flower.

In 1861, Texas Rangers raided Chief Nocona's camp. Nocona and Quanah escaped, but the Rangers captured both Cynthia Ann and Prairie Flower. The Rangers took them back to the Parker family. Unhappy with her relatives, Cynthia Ann tried several times to escape with Prairie Flower and rejoin the Quadhada Comanche, but they were always caught and returned. Prairie Flower died at ten years of age. Her mother died a few years later in 1874.

When the Comanche wars ended in 1875, Cynthia Ann's son, Quanah, now chief, lived on the reservation in Western Oklahoma. In order to survive he adopted white ways and urged all Comanche to do the same.

As he grew older, Quanah often thought about his mother and sister. He went to find their graves. He found his mother's grave in Texas and had her remains moved to Comanche County in Oklahoma. No one ever found Prairie Flower's grave.

Buffalo soldiers with "A" troop of the 10th Cavalry. Institute of Texan Cultures illustration no. 75-299

The warriors attacked the Toribio, Charco Escondido, and Soledad ranches and took 150–200 horses, weapons, money, clothes, blankets, and camp gear. The raiders killed at least forty-six people. A posse out of San Diego, Texas, gave chase and requested assistance that never arrived from the two thousand U.S. Cavalry troops stationed nearby. When the raiders reached the Rio Grande, they built makeshift rafts of wood. Along with their stolen goods and horses, the raiders floated across the Rio Grande and reached the safety of northern Mexico.

From 1875 to 1881, Black Seminole scouts led cavalry raiding parties against Indian tribes. At the Battle of Eagle's Nest Crossing on the Pecos River the army won, and John Ward, Isaac Payne, and Pompey Factor each received a Medal of Honor for their heroic actions in battle.

Also important in the army's efforts to stop the Indian raids were the Ninth and Tenth Cavalry regiments of African American troops. Following the Civil War many African Americans joined the military and were sent west to assist in the campaign against the Indi-

ans. The Indians respectfully called the black troopers "buffalo soldiers" because their hair reminded the Indians of buffalo fur. The
Indians considered the animal sacred and to be called a "buffalo
soldier" was an honor.[6]

By 1881, the army had killed many of the Texas Indians and forced
the survivors onto the reservations. The native people suffered on
the reservations. They suffered not only from their loss of freedom,
but also from poor food and medical care.

Reformers tried to help the Indians on the reservations. The
Women's National Indian Association and the Indians Rights Association organized to help in 1882, but they emphasized "civilizing"
the Indians. Civilizing meant turning the hard-riding, mobile, and
disciplined people into peaceful tax-paying farmers.[7] The people of
the Plains tribes did not make good farmers. They had lived a life of
almost constant movement following the buffaloes. They did not
want the settled life of a farmer. Other tribes adapted more easily to
farming on a reservation, but "civilizing" also meant education and
Christianizing, which the Indian people continued to resist.

CHAPTER 4
From Survival to Revival

Jaxon 02

THE REMAINING NATIVE PEOPLE in Texas suffered into the twentieth century. The government forced most Indians into Oklahoma, and only a few stayed in the Lone Star State. In 1900, only 470 people in Texas claimed Indian ancestry, and almost all lived in poverty. By the 1920 census, there were 2,109 Indians, and the poverty remained. By 1940 the number had dropped to 1,103. In 1960, there were 4,101 with most still living in poverty.

During the entire first half of the twentieth century, most of the native peoples in Texas lived on land allotted by the government, or they lived in small isolated rural settlements far from the economic activity and job opportunities of the urban areas. Additionally, most of them lived isolated from others of similar tribal origin. When they spoke publicly and asked for help, no one listened.

By the middle of the twentieth century, as the rural exodus to the city continued, many of the native people moved to Texas cities where they hoped to find jobs, better health care, and better schools for their children.

By 1960, as mentioned, most Texas Indians lived in urban centers while only 1,649 resided in rural areas. More recently, the Indian population has increased: 40,075 in 1980 and 65,877 in 1990. By 1995, the estimated Native American population in the state had grown to 84,000 with 43,000 men and 41,000 women. In 2000, the total number stood at 118,362. Overall, then, the native population in Texas increased from 470 in 1900 to 118,362 in 2000.

In part, the increased population of Texas Indians can be ex-

Tom Threepersons, Lawman

▼▼▼

Tom Threepersons became a legend in El Paso. Born a Cherokee on the reservation in Vinita, Oklahoma, on July 22, 1889, his mother supposedly named him "Threepersons" because she saw three men outside the day he was born.

As a young man, Tom served as a civilian scout for Gen. "Black Jack" Pershing's expedition into Mexico trailing Pancho Villa. When the mission ended, Tom found work at Fort Bliss breaking and training wild horses.

When the army cut its personnel in 1920, he found work with the government. During Prohibition, 1920–29, the six-foot, 180-pound Tom worked for several government agencies, including the Federal Prohibition Service, the

Tom Threepersons. Institute of Texan Cultures illustration

plained by the native people on the Oklahoma reservations moving back to Texas. They settled primarily in urban areas like Dallas–Fort Worth, Houston, San Antonio, and El Paso. Some of the increase was attributed to more mixed-blood Native Americans reclaiming their Indian heritage. Years ago, many people wanted to hide their native roots because of the prejudice and discrimination against them.

By the 1980s, the federal government had established programs that allowed Indian people to relocate, acquire job-training skills, and find jobs. In the early twenty-first century, members of some forty tribes claimed Texas as their home. The most numerous were those from the historic Five Civilized Tribes: the Cherokees numbered approximately 16,000; the Choctaws, about 8,000; the Chickasaws, around 2,300; about 2,200 Creeks; and approximately 550 Seminoles. Other tribes with at least 1,000 included the Apaches with 2,200; the Sioux with 1,600; the Comanches with 1,500; and the Pueblos or Tiguas with about 1,400. All the numbers were probably undercounts as many native people still greatly feared census takers and refused to report information to the government. Three tribes have reservation land in Texas: the Alabama-Coushattas, the Kickapoos, and the Tiguas.[1] By 2000, the Alabama-Coushattas numbered approximately 1,300; the Tiguas about 1,400; and the Kickapoos about 650.

By 2001, approximately 40,000 native people lived in the Dallas–Fort Worth metropolitan area while San Antonio and Houston also continued to have increases in their Indian populations. Urban Indians struggled to find time from jobs to maintain their remembered traditions. Such traditions included both the social pow-wows where many tribal peoples come together as well as the ceremonies of individual tribes on the reservations.

In the city, newly arrived Native Americans experienced great uncertainty and confusion. The Indian people missed their families and felt ripped away from their traditions and culture. But, still, they came to cities for jobs, an education, and, hopefully, a more prosperous life.

U.S. Customs Service, the El Paso Sheriff's Office, and the El Paso Police. Always in the front-line shootouts fighting to stop the illegal smuggling of alcohol from Mexico, his guns became famous.

In one fight, he arrested a smuggler crossing the Rio Grande, but he soon was surrounded by more armed smugglers. In the fight, he fired forty rounds from his rifle. Running out of ammunition, he retreated just as help arrived. The authorities rounded up the smugglers and captured thirteen five-gallon cans of alcohol; seventy-nine pints and twenty-five quarts of tequila; two pints of beer; three quarts of cognac; and twelve pints of whiskey.

The Mexican smugglers put a $10,000 reward for anyone who would kill Tom. No one ever collected the reward.

▼▼▼

Comanche Code-Talkers

▼▼▼

During World War II Comanche men served as "code-talkers." Navajo code-talkers served in the Pacific theatre during World War II, but few know about the Comanche code-talkers who served in the European theatre. As descendants of the Comanches who once roamed the Panhandle and West Texas, the code-talkers relayed information using their language as a code that our enemies neither understood nor could learn to understand. The enemy never broke the Indian codes.

The contributions of the Comanche talkers remain unknown by most Americans even though a recent movie highlighted their contribution to the war effort. The French government, however, recognized the Comanche talkers in

The federal government established an urban relocation program designed to help Indians overcome generations of poverty. In 1952, the Bureau of Indian Affairs (BIA) established an Employment Assistance Program. The government paid the moving expenses for Indians willing to migrate to urban areas. The government also started a job-training program and gave program participants enough money to pay at least one month's bills.

In addition, the government helped Indian people find jobs and housing. The BIA provided one year of free medical care. In 1957, the government added an Adult Vocational Training Program. It also began spending more money for education. As a result, more Indians entered colleges. Yet the urban life was still a very difficult one for many Indians.

Susan Johnson, a Kiowa, grew up in a small town, Mountain View, Oklahoma. She had a troubled childhood that included alcohol abuse. She married and moved with her husband to Dallas to start a new life. But she experienced white people insulting her, calling her "squaw" and her husband "chief." Susan felt that people did not respect each other or their different religions. Her husband told her to be cold and hard. He said that it was a "dog-eat-dog" world and that she must get used to it.

Tigua men roofing a building during a construction project. Institute of Texan Cultures illustration no. 76-46

▼▼▼

1989 by awarding them the French National Order of Merit for "outstanding" and "meritorious" services during the war.

Charles Chibitty served as a Comanche code-talker. As he attended pow-wows throughout 2000, he was honored as an American hero. His war service is a reminder of the important work being done by native peoples who strive to preserve their native languages today. On February 10, 2001, Chibitty was inducted into the Oklahoma Military Hall of Fame.

Elmer Sugar Brown takes part in many pow-wows across the country. Institute of Texan Cultures illustration no. 3515A

The Dallas office of the Bureau of Indian Affairs in 1974. Institute of Texan Cultures illustration no. 76-47

When she first moved to Dallas, Susan had trouble with everyday problems. She had to ride buses and the bus schedules confused her. She had problems using the telephone. When the family car needed repair, Susan and her husband had to take the car to a stranger found in the telephone book. Susan missed her Oklahoma family and returned often to visit them.

Gregory Gonzales, a Mescalero Lipan Apache, also moved to Dallas. He had an easier time adjusting to city life than Susan Johnson. In many ways, he remained a "cultural" Indian. He gave his two children Apache names. He waited until they were old enough to understand and then told them the tribal legends. Like Susan's husband, people called Gonzales "chief." He believed that many people were ignorant and that some people were actually trying to show respect by calling him "chief." He felt they wanted to acknowledge his Indian heritage.

Dianna Begaye Vaca lived on the Navajo reservation in New Mexico before moving to Dallas. She had attended a New Mexico college with a majority of Navajo students. After she married, she moved to Dallas with her husband. In Dallas, she experienced "culture shock" and insecurity, as she had never been around so many white people. While her husband was at work, Dianna felt alone and isolated. The behavior of some whites shocked Dianna. Some Anglos thought that as a Native American, she had special powers to reach the "spirit world." Other people believed that she should be able to predict the future. Most were surprised that she did not have "visions." She did not fit their idea of what an Indian was supposed to be. Dianna said that whites believe Indians are "frozen in time."

Sharon Warshield, a Southern Cheyenne, originally lived in Watonga, a small town in northwestern Oklahoma. When she was a child, her father moved the family to Dallas where he got a better job. Sharon attended a Dallas high school. Hispanic students thought she was a Hispanic, too, and spoke Spanish to her. She did not know the language, and they were insulted when she was silent. They decided that she was "stuck-up." When the Hispanics learned that Sharon was a Native American, that was even worse. They did not like Indians.

Sandra Newheart's parents moved to Dallas before she was born. Sandra's mixed heritage included Creek, Chickasaw, Delaware, and Shawnee. Sandra grew up in the urban environment. She grew up "white" even though others often mistook her for Hispanic. She attended urban schools and had no trouble adjusting. Dallas was the only home that she knew. She took pride in her Native American heritage and practiced some of the traditional ways.

By 2001, Dallas had an Inter-tribal Center where native people went for assistance. Counselors helped with practical problems like finding a place to live, understanding bus schedules, and finding jobs. When health problems developed, the counselors helped to find the right doctors. Sometimes the center helped by providing food until a job was found.

A relatively recent development in the Dallas–Fort Worth Metroplex area was the "Pan-Indian" movement. Tribes were encouraged to unite to address the poverty and other problems faced by many native peoples in America. Dallas had a strong "Pan-Indian" movement with social clubs open to all native peoples. There were

"Pan-Indian" softball and basketball teams, golf tournaments, and bowling leagues. The various events allowed all Native Americans in the area to come together for pleasure, support, and camaraderie.

By 2002, the urban Native Americans also celebrated some of their old traditions with public pow-wows open to dancers, drummers, and singers of all tribes. Each tribe had its own particular songs and dances. All participants were given a chance to perform songs and dances of their own unique culture. The pow-wows featured feasting and socializing.

Indians worried about losing their heritage since many ceremonies and rituals were already forgotten. As individuals died, rituals often died with them. Languages ceased to be used, and many tribal words could not be translated into English. Native languages were essential in carrying on tribal rituals. Stories passed on for generations could not be shared with grandchildren living a different life in a city. The uniquely different cultures had begun to blur.

To help Native Americans preserve their cultures, Ruth E. Smith founded the American Indian Heritage Center in Dallas. Established to help retain the history and heritage of all Texas Indians, its Sequoyah House Gallery showcases Native American paintings, sculptures, and a variety of handmade craft items. The Center also sponsors an annual art contest, the Star Charity Rodeo, the "Cynthia Ann Parker Days," which honors Chief Quanah Parker's white mother and gives the Ira Hayes Award. Ira Hayes was a courageous Pima who fought in World War II. The annual award goes to a young cadet engaged in military training in a Texas high school.

Despite the number of government programs throughout the twentieth century, the Native Americans in Texas were almost an invisible minority when compared to other minority groups. Most governmental programs went to other more visible or vocal groups such as blacks and Hispanics. Programs offered did not meet the unique needs of the native populations. The federal Senior Community Service Employment Program started in 1965 as part of President Johnson's efforts to abolish poverty in America. Yet Indians as an identifiable group never participated in the program.

▼▼▼

Cynthia Ann Parker holding Prairie Flower, 1862. Institute of Texan Cultures illustration no. 68-80

In 1989 the National Indian Council on Aging campaigned hard for inclusion in new legislation. The government included Native Americans, and the council's Dallas administrator, Gerri Norton, obtained seventy-four salaried positions for elderly Indians who wanted to work. Such programs allowed many elderly native people to at least reach an economic subsistence level to take care of themselves.

Like their nineteenth- and early-twentieth-century ancestors, urban Indians struggled to hold onto their Native American heritage. It was part of their identity. Some progress has occurred. Indeed, survival has led to revival.[2]

THE ALABAMA-COUSHATTAS

Near Livingston, in Polk County just on the edges of the Big Thicket in East Texas, live the Alabama-Coushattas. Originally from Alabama, the Alabama-Coushattas once lived in the southeastern woodlands.

According to the folklore, God made the Alabama-Coushattas from clay, and they lived in a large underground cave. Their trip from the cave to the earth's surface was a long one. They camped three nights along the way and finally reached the entrance. They saw a big tree standing at the hole that exited the underground. The Alabamas left the cave on one side of the tree, and the Coushattas left by the other side. That is why to this day the two peoples have slightly different languages yet still live with each other as relatives.

The people ventured out of the cave only at night. One night they became alarmed when they heard a hooting owl, a sound that they had never heard before. Most of the people ran back into the underground and never left again. This explains why there were so few Alabama-Coushattas. If the old owl had been quiet and had not scared so many in hiding, the Alabama-Coushattas would be a big tribe today.

Like many peoples, including Jews and Christians, the Alabama-Coushattas believed a great flood covered the Earth at one time. In the Alabama-Coushatta tale, a youngster of their tribe rescued a frog from a fire. The grateful frog could see the future and decided to help the young man and his people. The frog said that heavy rains would come and that water would soon cover all the Earth. The frog told the youngster to make a big raft if he wanted the Alabama-Coushattas to survive. When the young man told his people about the frog's prediction, everyone just laughed, but the youngster built a big raft. When the flood came the young man saved many of his people along with many of the Earth's animals. And that is why the Alabama-Coushattas survived as a tribe to this day.

Historians say that the Coushattas came to Texas in the 1790s and settled near the Big Thicket. About one thousand Alabamas

joined them in 1805. The Alabamas established Peach Tree village in today's Tyler County, where they built log cabins and lived as farmers, hunters, and fishermen. Over time, the two tribes intermarried and became one tribe: Alabama-Coushattas.

The Alabama-Coushattas believed in more than one god, with the sun as the supreme God, until Presbyterian missionaries arrived. The missionaries converted most of Alabama-Coushattas to Christianity. Today, the Presbyterian Church has the largest membership within the tribe.

Early tribal government included rule by a principal chief and a second chief chosen for lifetime terms by tribal members. The chiefs and the tribal council settled disputes.

In the 1830s, the Republic of Texas gave each tribe two leagues of land, about 8,000 acres, along the Trinity River. But soon, whites began settling in the area and taking the tribes' land. President Sam Houston persuaded the Texas Congress to buy 1,280 acres to replace

The Presbyterian Church built about 1890 on the Alabama-Coushatta Reservation. Institute of Texan Cultures illustration no. 72-1732

Students at the first Alabama-Coushatta school in Livingston, Texas, 1911. Institute of Texan Cultures illustration no. 72-1694

the lost land. The new land, however, could sustain neither farming nor grazing cattle and horses. The men scavenged in the Big Thicket hoping to find enough food for their families. The tribes almost perished from starvation and disease. The population that had been about one thousand was reduced to only two hundred. The tribes lived on their unproductive land for almost a hundred years without assistance from anyone.

In the 1940s the state and federal governments gave some help. The government bought more than 3,100 acres next to the original land grant where the tribes lived. Tribal members were finally able to move from aging log cabins into wood frame houses. The government also paid more attention to the health and the education of the people.

New Indian policy of the federal government in the 1950s withdrew federal supervision of all tribes and established a policy known as "termination." The Dwight D. Eisenhower administration renounced federal involvement with the Native Americans. As a result, the state government took over with the permission of the Alabama-Coushatta Tribal Council. In 1957, a Tribal Council became the major governing agency of the two tribes. The people elected seven members to the council while still retaining a principal chief and a second chief, with the latter handling many of the day-to-day tribal issues.

Also in 1957, the state granted management of the timber industry on the reservation to the council. The council took great care to conserve the forest from over-cutting and cooperated with the Texas Forest Service. The money earned from the sales of the timber paid for many projects that benefited the Alabama-Coushatta tribal members. In 1959, the state allowed the council to lease mineral rights on their land, which brought some additional money into the tribes' treasury. Most of the new money went for improvements in education for the young and college scholarships.

Despite the progress being made, problems continued. Beyond the timber and the mineral leases, little economic development occurred on the reservation, and there were no jobs. To improve the job opportunities, the Tribal Council turned to the tourist industry. Helped by the state, the tribes built a restaurant, a gift shop, and a museum in 1963. They also held public tribal square dances and

The first two Alabama-Coushatta to attend Durant College in Sherman, Texas, c. 1929. Institute of Texan Cultures illustration no. 72-1706

McConico Battise, Alabama-Coushatta, c. 1928. Institute of Texan Cultures illustration no. 72-1699

gave tours through the Big Thicket. In 1971, engineers developed Lake Tombigbee, a twenty-six-acre lake where tourists camp, swim, ski, fish, and picnic. By the beginning of the twenty-first century, more than 200,000 people visited the tribes' homeland each year.

The jobs created by tourism helped the tribes tremendously. Since the 1970s, brick homes have replaced the older frame houses. In the 1980s, the Tribal Council petitioned to become a federally recognized tribe, and President Ronald Reagan signed the law in 1987. With the new status the tribes qualified for federal assistance to help construct a new health clinic, to get head start programs for the younger children, and to participate in other federal programs.

By 2000, the Alabama and the Coushatta had begun to address concerns about the preservation of their traditional language. Elders like Zetha Battise held language classes as well as traditional craft classes in weaving pine needle baskets and making pottery and other handcrafts.

In 2000, sixty-seven-year-old Chief Clayton Sylvestine, a descendant of Chief Cooper Sylvestine, worked in the old way. He still made trips into the Big Thicket, swinging a machete to cut river cane. He gathered pine needles for weaving baskets tight enough to hold water. The reservation gift shop sold the chief's baskets along with crafts produced by other tribal members.

Alabama-Coushatta adults knew that much of their culture had been lost. They knew little of their ancestors who worshiped the Sun God. Christian missionaries suppressed their gods and declared native dances paganistic. But a few courageous people kept some knowledge of the ceremonial dances alive. The few traditions remembered have been transferred to the children and grandchildren. By 2002, there had been a revival of the traditional dances.

The Alabama-Coushattas strictly enforced their tribal membership codes. They were equally strict about who could live on their reservation. One must be a full blood to belong to the tribe, and anyone who marries people outside the tribe cannot live on the reservation. The Alabamas and Coushattas numbered about 1,300 to 1,400 people in 2000. They have lived on their reservation continuously since the 1850s when Republic of Texas President Sam Houston got the state to make the land available. With the purchase of additional land with tribal monies, the reservation encompassed about 4,700 acres in 2000.

Despite progress, the tribe still had a housing shortage and high unemployment. They established a casino on their reservation to further improve economic conditions. New houses popped up. Tribal members purchased better cars. Workmen repaired their Native American Church. Adults even talked of one day being able to pay college tuition for all their young people who wanted to attend.[3]

THE TIGUAS

Ysleta del Sur is the oldest continuously settled town in the Lone Star State. The native people fashioned a way of life similar to the life they had lived in New Mexico. Escaping with the Spanish during the Pueblo Revolt they were converted to Catholicism and built the mission Corpus Christi de la Ysleta in 1682. It remains the oldest mission in Texas.

By year 2002, the Tiguas of Ysleta, Texas, found it difficult to maintain their culture and their way of life. First, Spaniards introduced changes such as the Catholic Church and the Spanish language. Then came the Mexican presence combining the cultures of the Spaniards and the Indians of Mexico. Still later, white and black Americans migrated to the El Paso area and introduced elements of their culture.

By the 1930s, many experts believed that the Tiguas were a vanished tribe. Many people in the tribe had become Hispanicized. They married into Mexican American families and took Hispanic names. They adopted the Spanish language and Mexican dress. Additionally, the tribe did not perform their ceremonies in public. They tried to hide their "Indianness" to escape the prejudice and bigotry. The experts were mistaken about the continued existence of the tribe, but the people faced severe financial problems.

▼▼▼

The Tigua lived in poverty in their old neighborhood, the Barrio de los Indios. The poverty continued though the 1930s and 1940s. In the mid-1950s, conditions became even worse when the city of El Paso annexed the town of Ysleta, home of the impoverished Tiguas. The annexation meant that each family would have to pay property taxes of about one hundred dollars per year. The yearly average income for Tigua families was about $400. They could not afford the taxes.

The Tiguas fought the new tax by saying they lived on land that was exempt from taxation. They claimed that their ownership came as a result of an old Spanish land grant. The grant stated that the land could not be taxed. Various Spanish and Mexican documents proved the Tiguas correct. The tribe's spokesmen also called attention to the Treaty of Guadalupe Hidalgo in which the United States promised to honor the old Spanish land grants.

To secure federal aid, though, the Tigua still had to prove their culture had existed continuously since the earliest days of European contact. The Tiguas' attorney, Tom Diamond, a champion of Indian

Home on the Tigua Reservation, c. 1970. Institute of Texan Cultures illustration no. 73-317E

Tigua in ceremonial dress posed in front of pueblo in 1936. Institute of Texan Cultures illustration no. 68-50A

rights, proved that the Tigua descended from the Pueblo tribes of New Mexico. But the federal government continued to study the issue while the tribe's people remained in poverty.

As late as 1960, no tribal member had ever attended college, and no tribal member had ever graduated from high school. Tigua children did not go to school because they had no shoes. The children felt humiliated. The principal chief made his living picking cotton. In 1965, only one Tigua home had utilities such as electricity, gas, and water. Many of the Tiguas still lived in mesquite and brush jacales or huts. Women baked in *hornos,* a dome-shaped adobe outdoor oven.

During the reform era of the 1960s, Tiguas reasserted themselves. As Blacks, women, Hispanics, and other groups demanded their rights as Americans, Indians did too. In 1961, President John F.

Kennedy promised justice for the Native Americans. Secretary of the Interior Stewart Udall appointed a commission chaired by the chief of the Cherokee Nation to study Indian problems. The commission recommended that the federal government do more to help Native Americans overcome handicaps that prior government policies had created by forcing them onto reservations.

When Lyndon B. Johnson became president in 1963, he referred to the Indians as the "forgotten Americans." In the 1960s, an Indian could expect to live only about forty-four years while the average white life expectancy was about seventy years. Native Americans had the highest infant mortality, alcoholism, and tuberculosis rates in the United States. Native Americans died from pneumonia and influenza three times more frequently than non-Indians. The Indian suicide rate was six times higher than any other group in the country.

All studies of the native people still stressed poverty and overcrowded households. Most Native Americans continued to live in a cycle of poverty from one generation to the next. Reports also showed that school officials spent government money meant for Indian education on other priorities. In the public schools, the

Young Tigua men carry the statue of their patron saint, St. Anthony, c. 1992. Institute of Texan Cultures illustration no. 92-369, neg. 86-25, no. 30, courtesy of Bill Wright

▼▼▼

Indian dropout rate exceeded 50 percent. And the Tigua were among the poorest of all.

In 1967, the state of Texas recognized the Tigua as an Indian tribe. Influenced by President Johnson, the federal government granted official tribal recognition. The action recognized the tribe's twenty-six acres as a reservation. With tribal status the Tigua began receiving federal and state aid for improved housing and health benefits, including programs to fight alcoholism. They built new housing in the multistory pueblo-style. About 1,400 tribal members lived there in 1995.

In the school, teachers taught classes in Tigua history and heritage. To offer classes in the Tewa language, though, teachers had to be imported from New Mexico pueblos because no Texas Tigua could teach such a course. But within a few years, Tigua teachers taught the language courses with older Tiguas passing along remembered oral traditions.

The Ysleta Del Sur Cultural Center and Pueblo Museum, southeast of El Paso, opened in 1975. Housed in the historic Alderette-Candelaria house, built in 1840, Tigua staff present information about the history and culture of the Tiguas. Fiesta de San Antonio held annually in June remains one of the Tigua's biggest celebrations. Tiguas perform ceremonial dances with the traditional drumming and chanting.

The Tiguas continued to be governed by a cacique, a religious leader elected for life by the tribal council. Men of the tribe elected the tribal council. A war chief could also be elected if warfare threatened.

By 2000, many Tiguas worked for the tribe. Others lived and worked in the larger El Paso community. The Tiguas numbered at least 1,400 in 2001 and as a result of their casino were experiencing prosperity.

In 1993, the tribe opened the Speaking Rock Casino in El Paso. The casino was located less than one hundred yards from the old Ysleta mission. By the late 1990s, profits from the casino amounted to more than $60 million a year. The money helped the Tigua get

Tigua chiefs Cacique Damaso Colmenero (second from left) and Aldelantodo Cleofas Calleros (far right), c. 1930. Institute of Texan Cultures illustration no. 71-362

improved medical care, better housing, and sufficient food. Leaders used some of the profits for education. The Tiguas generously gave the Catholic Church $100,000 for the renovation and the rebuilding of the old mission. Economic expansion continued, and by 2000, the Tigua unemployment rate had fallen from 50 percent to 1 percent. The casino made annual payments to tribal members averaging $20,000 for each man, woman, and child registered in the Tigua Nation. The children's money went into trust funds. The casino money also funded a new housing project, a library, and a swimming pool. Any Tigua student who wanted to go to college received a full scholarship.

In 1998, the Tiguas bought a 68,000-acre ranch for $9 million. The acreage was located in Jeff Davis and Presidio Counties and was rich in Tigua history and culture. The tribe used it for a recreational area and to conduct certain religious rites. The gambling casino allowed the Tiguas to end the cycle of poverty.[4] But the gaming for all Texas tribes remained an issue as the state moved in 2002 to shut down casinos.

▼▼▼

Ysleta mission, June 13, 1962. Institute of Texan Cultures illustration no. 71-383

THE KICKAPOOS

The Kickapoos once lived in the Great Lakes region. French explorers encountered them in the 1640s. After conflicts with the Iroquois over hunting grounds, the Kickapoos moved into the land of Wisconsin and continued to trade with the French. Seminomadic, the Kickapoos lived in villages part of the year where they planted and harvested crops. After planting, they broke into small groups and hunted for wild game on the prairies.

As white or pioneer settlers moved west the Kickapoo were forced to relocate. By the 1830s, the tribe had been forced southward to Oklahoma and Texas. Because of the frequent relocations, there developed deep divisions among the Kickapoos, or Kiikaapoa as they called themselves. In time, three Kickapoo factions became virtually independent of each other: the Kansas Kickapoos, the Oklahoma Kickapoos, and the Mexican Kickapoos, also called the Texas Band of the Oklahoma Kickapoo. This band reached Mexican Texas around 1833 or 1834. They joined the alliance of migrant tribes living in northeast Texas with Cherokee Chief Bowl. The Army of the Republic of Texas drove them out of Texas in 1839. Members of the Texas band fled either into Mexico or into today's Oklahoma.

Many members of the Texas Kickapoos went to Nacimiento, Mexico. There, they mingled with other Indians in northern Mexico and became raiders into the Lone Star State. Kickapoos from Kansas and Oklahoma later joined the Texas band in Mexico. The war-

Tigua children playing, c. 1992. Institute of Texan Cultures illustration no. 92-369, neg. 87-8, no. 29, courtesy of Bill Wright

Kickapoo wickiup homes in Nacimiento, Mexico, in 1936. Institute of Texan Cultures illustration no. 77-158

riors continued their raids throughout the Civil War era. The raiders suffered defeats in the 1870s after a new line of forts were built and the military patrolled the Rio Grande, so the Texas band of Kickapoos remained in Mexico.

In the early 1890s, many of the Oklahoma Kickapoos left Indian Territory because the missionaries would not stop trying to convert them to Christianity. Some of the Oklahoma Kickapoos simply refused to give up their native religion. So they left and joined the Texas band of Kickapoos in Mexico.

The Kickapoos remained a self-reliant and independent people. They often refused to acknowledge outside authority or let other people give them orders. Even into the modern era, they held fast to their religion and traditional ways. They educated their young according to their old ways, not as outsiders wanted. And the tribe never performed their ceremonies in public.

To remain true to their heritage, the tribal members spoke in their traditional Algonquian tongue. They used Spanish or English only when necessary. They lived in traditional housing called wickiups or wigwams. The men made the housing from wood and woven mats, with tree bark covering the roofs. The women supervised construction.

The Texas or Mexican band developed a unique relationship with both the United States and Mexico. Generally, they traveled wherever they pleased, paying little attention to the official border between Mexico and the United States. Even into the 1980s and 1990s, they crossed and recrossed the border at will. They continued to live near Nacimiento, Mexico, about ninety miles south of Eagle Pass during the winter. There, they performed their winter religious rituals and planted their traditional crops of corn, sweet potatoes, beans, pumpkins, and squash. The women did most of the farming and gathering of wild foods. The men hunted wild game such as deer, bears, rabbits, and squirrels.

When the warm months came, the Kickapoo migrated north. In early spring, observers found them in Texas living under the north side of the International Bridge that links Piedras Negras, Mexico, and Eagle Pass, Texas. They called their village "Little Heart." The Kickapoo people have come to "Little Heart" every year since the 1940s. It was a place where they raised their children and buried their dead. They lived there next to a lush golf course. As the whites

A Kickapoo family in front of their wickiup about 1900. Institute of Texan Cultures illustration no. 77-166

Nakai Breen

▼▼▼

The Kickapoo called her "Unakah," meaning "the bark that protects the tree." Nakai, a full-blooded Cherokee, was born in Stillwell, Oklahoma. At the age of seven she was sent to Eagle Pass, Texas, where a local family adopted her.

When Nakai was twelve years old she was on her way to school when she saw a Kickapoo elder and her husband knocking on a door. A Spanish-speaking woman answered and the Kickapoo woman asked in sign language for a cup of coffee. The home owner slammed the door in their faces. Nakai met the Kickapoo woman and took her and her husband home with her. So began Nakai's determination to help the Kickapoos. From 1942 to 1986, she focused all of her efforts to assist them.

Kickapoo chiefs at Musquiz, Mexico, in 1900. Institute of Texan Cultures illustration no. 77-423

played golf, the nearby Kickapoo lived in squalor. They had one water spigot for their forty cardboard and cane hovels. During the harvest season, they often worked as migrant agricultural laborers.

In 1983, the state government attempted to resolve the question of Kickapoo citizenship. The state gave the group land near Indio, Texas. Hoping to make the Kickapoo eligible for federal aid, the state also tried to get tribal recognition from the federal government. In 1985, the Kickapoo became citizens of the United States. Immigration officials issued citizenship certificates to 143 tribal members, about one-third of the 650-member tribe. Two Kickapoo refused citizenship and received status as permanent resident aliens. In effect, the Kickapoo have dual citizenship recognized by both Mexico and the United States. They qualified for federal benefits such as health care and food stamps. As recently as 2002, they still spent time in both countries.

Into the 1990s, the Kickapoo were living in poverty. They still depended on federal or state welfare programs for assistance. Then

▼▼▼

Nakai Breen. Courtesy of Nakai Breen

When she first began to learn about the Kickapoo, Nakai found them living under the International Bridge in Eagle Pass, Texas. Wanting to assist them, Nakai learned to communicate with them using sign language, and later she learned to speak their Kickapoo language.

She saw the terrible results of poverty. She saw disease caused by malnutrition. She saw the difficulty of life without running water and proper sewage. She saw people abusing alcohol. She saw the lack of medical care because sick Kickapoos had no money. When possible, she either used her own funds or borrowed from others so that hospital bills could be paid.

For forty-five years Nakai worked with the Kickapoo to assist them in bettering their lives. She fought for their right to be recognized as

American citizens, and as a representative, she testified before the U.S. Congress and Senate on their behalf. Her efforts proved successful. In 1985, they were granted U.S. citizenship, which provided them access to the services provided by the government.

She worked with the Catholic and Presbyterian Churches as well as individual donors to raise money in order to buy a 125-acre reservation near Eagle Pass, Texas. The Kickapoo Reservation held in trust by the Federal Government continues today.

Nakai Breen at seventy-two years old served as the founder and director of a multicultural educational center and museum located in Brackettville, Texas. She continued to serve the people even into the new millenium.

in 1996, they opened the Lucky Eagle Casino in Eagle Pass. Almost immediately, the tribe began to prosper. The Southwest Casino and Hotel Corporation managed the Lucky Eagle. The corporation had an agreement with the National Indian Gaming Commission created by Congress in 1988. The commission's job was to protect Native Americans everywhere from organized crime and other corrupting influences. The commission also ensured that the profits benefited the tribes engaged in such enterprises.

The casino profits provided money for health care, education, housing, and food. With better health the tribal population grew to eight hundred members by 1998. That year, the casino had 147 employees, 40 percent of which were Kickapoo. By May of 2001, four hundred Kickapoo had employment at the casino.

In 1998, Texas Governor George W. Bush sued the tribe, claiming casino gambling illegal in Texas. Bush wanted to close existing casino operations. The Kickapoo, Tigua, and Alabama-Coushatta all cried foul. They pointed to the state-sponsored lottery, the biggest gambling game in the Lone Star State. The Kickapoo and other Native American tribes believed that if the state could gamble, then federally recognized Indians could, too.

Meanwhile, the Texas Kickapoo continued to follow their traditions. Family remained very important and they took kinship responsibilities seriously. Anyone in trouble could turn to relatives for help. Generally, the Kickapoo still married within the tribe and resisted formal education. They feared "white" education would undermine the tribe and its traditions as it had done in other tribes. Nevertheless, some younger members of the Texas band started going to public schools. Increasingly, the Kickapoo, especially the young, came under the influences of the modern era. Radio, television, movies, and the ongoing computer revolution had their effects. But collectively the Texas Kickapoo band remained one of the most traditional of America's native peoples.[5]

▼▼▼

NATIVE AMERICAN ISSUES

Beyond gaming rights and land issues, Native American controversies continued into the twenty-first century. The portrayal of the native people in Texas history textbooks used in the schools upset many Indian people. The authors of Texas history textbooks tried to avoid taking biased views. The Texas State Board of Education required that all people be treated fairly. Books adopted by the State Board were to note the positive contributions of all groups in the development of modern Texas. Still, most textbooks emphasized the accomplishments of white people, especially white men.

Other problems existed. For example, in 1999, a major state newspaper editor complained that depictions of Confederate heroes and symbols dominated the state's monuments. Confederate heroes also dominated most historical photograph collections. In 2001, Texas Legislator Ron Wilson complained that upon seeing all the Confederate monuments, one would think that white men single-handedly built the Lone Star State and then won the Civil War. Wilson wanted more fair play. He thought that African Americans, Hispanics, and Native Americans should be represented in the state's monuments. Wilson and his supporters said that glorifying one group distorted the history and the unique diversity and pluralism of the Lone Star State.[6]

Cultural misunderstandings continued to plague the Lone Star State. In a 1992 incident, the Apache Itsa-Licii, or Golden Eagle Gomez, of Mesquite allowed his hair to grow long and wore it in braids. Golden Eagle's father also wore his hair long. Apache boys and men traditionally wore their hair long. The Apaches' native religion includes numerous beliefs about hair. But when Golden Eagle enrolled in the first grade, there was trouble. The Mesquite School District had a twenty-five-year-old rule about hair length. A boy's hair had to be short enough to stay out of his eyes, and the back had to be above his shirt collar. School authorities allowed Golden Eagle to enroll until they made a decision about his hair length. The board members did not change the old policy; the hair policy stood. The board expelled first grader Itsa-Licii.

Similar problems occurred elsewhere in Texas. In Lubbock, the parents of an Indian student filed a legal suit. They wanted a judge to overturn Lubbock's hair length policy. The parents lost. In one South Texas urban area, a Chippewa woman with long hair worked as a registered nurse. She applied for a job with the local school. The school district's board denied her employment because she would not cut her hair. Critics of such hair length policies accused school authorities of violating the U.S. Constitution because the Constitution allows freedom of religion.[7]

Other struggles have developed about the use of Indian symbols and words for mascots of the state's schools. At Keller High School, north of Fort Worth, football cheerleaders wore beaded headbands and students did the "tomahawk chop" during games. At Port Neches Groves High School, the "Indian Spirit" was the mascot. The Indian Spirit carried an Indian shield and feather-covered spear and did war dances during football games. The football scoreboard read "Welcome to the Reservation."

About forty other Texas schools were named the "Indians." Others had such names as Redskins, Braves, Apaches, Comanches, and Indian Arrows. State universities and colleges such as McMurray in Abilene and Midwestern State in Wichita Falls field teams called the "Indians." Over the years many Native American groups protested the use of the Indian names and symbols. From their perspective the use of such words belittles their history and culture. They felt humiliated and ashamed. The United States Commission on Civil Rights agreed. In 2001, the commission recommended that all non-Indian schools including secondary schools and colleges stop using Native American names and mascots. The commission believed the practice to be disrespectful and insulting.[8]

Conclusion

*A*S THE LONE STAR STATE entered a new millennium, native people could reflect on a long and rich history. Their ancestors were the first people to enter the Western Hemisphere. They spread their culture from today's Alaska to the tip of South America. Through time, those ancestors separated into many subgroups or tribes. Each developed its own, sometimes unique, culture based on the land and the environment.

The culture and daily life of many Indian people were very different from the Europeans who came to America. Indians view the land differently. Land is a gift given into our custody to tend and preserve for future generations and not something to be owned. The different views about land ownership lay at the core of many problems that developed between the Native Americans and the Europeans and later the Americans. The differences caused violent conflicts. That violence coupled with diseases killed thousands and almost destroyed the many native tribes. The differing beliefs about land continue in 2003 as cases about land, mineral, and water rights are brought before the courts. With legal settlement comes stability and pride as Indian people reclaim sacred lands and continue religious practices.

Many Native American tribes made decisions on what is best for the group rather than the individual. And leaders waited to make their decisions until nearly all reached agreement. The councils and chiefs did not make decisions quickly, and change came slowly.

Tigua women baking bread in hornos for a celebration, c. 1992. Institute of Texan Cultures illustration no. 92-369, neg. 91-10, courtesy of Bill Wright

Christianity and tribal spiritual beliefs existed side-by-side with no apparent inconsistencies. Like Indian warriors of the past, Native Americans continued to verbally fight for their rights as natives on this land. They asked the majority to allow them to live with beliefs that were obviously different from that majority whether it be hair length, the desecration of graves, or the federal government's accountability for their trust funds.

In the modern era, Texas Indians assumed control of their lives by moving from "survival" to "revival." Native Americans like the Tigua, the Kickapoo, and the Alabama-Coushatta have in part preserved and reclaimed aspects of their old culture. Like the Coahuiltecan, some tribes once thought extinct have miraculously survived and struggle to reclaim their heritage and identity. As recently as 1997, the Texas Legislature recognized the Tap Pilam-

▼▼▼

Coahuiltecan as a historic tribe, even though many experts had claimed that the Coahuiltecan no longer existed.

Indian gaming brought an end to the cycle of poverty endured for generations by native peoples. With better diets and improved medical care the native populations ended their population decline.

Many individuals were separated from their tribes. They moved into urban areas to find employment. They had little time to make trips home to participate in the extended ceremonial rituals. Yet many still practiced the old traditional ways as much as possible. Traditional native crafts made the "old" way commanded premium prices and remained a source of pride for Indian artisans.

Many mixed-blood Native Americans who once hid their "Indianness" now reclaimed that heritage. As survivors of a federal policy of genocide, the Indian people rightfully claimed a rich and noble heritage. Engulfed in tradition and ceremony based on the fertility of the land, the annual harvest cycles continued. Theirs is a gift and legacy that enriches us all, a people no longer invisible or forgotten. The story of our native peoples is a part of Texas history, forever.

Notes

CHAPTER 1. FROM PREHISTORY TO FOREIGN INVASIONS

1. For more details on the Archaic era, see Harry J. Shafer, *Ancient Texans: Rock Art and Lifeways along the Lower Pecos* (Houston: Gulf Publishing Company, 1992), pp. 86–88, 137, 158, 186, 209, 229; W. W. Newcomb, *The Indians of Texas: From Prehistoric to Modern Times* (Austin: Texas State Historical Association, 1969), pp. 15–19; David La Vere, *Life among the Texas Indians: The WPA Narratives* (College Station: Texas A&M University Press, 1998), pp. 5–6; Jules H. Billar, ed., *The World of the American Indian* (Washington, D.C.: The National Geographic Society, 1974), pp. 43–51; and Marshall Sahlins, "Notes on the Original Affluent Society," in *Man the Hunter*, ed. Richard B. Lee and Irven De Vore (Chicago: Aldine Publishing Company, 1968), pp. 85–89. Also see Leland C. Bement, *Hunter-Gatherer Mortuary Practices during the Texas Archaic* (Austin: University of Texas Press, 1994) and Donald Worthington, *Prehistoric Indians of the Southwest* (Denver: Denver Museum of Natural History, 1959), passim.

2. Shafer, *Ancient Texans*, pp. 138–89; Forrest Kirkland and W. W. Newcomb, *The Rock Art of Texas Indians* (Austin: University of Texas Press, 1967); Michael Doss, *The Indian Nations: The First Americans* (New York: Coordination Committee for Ellis Island, n.d.), pp. 1–2; La Vere, *Life among the Texas Indians*, pp. 5–6.

3. Carol Baldridge, *Texas Indians Fact Cards* (Milpitas, Calif.: Toucan Valley Publications, Inc., 1997), p. 30.

4. La Vere, *Life among the Texas Indians*, pp. 5–6; Timothy K. Perttula, *The Caddo Nation: Archaeological and Ethnohistoric Perspectives* (Austin: University of Texas Press, 1994), p. 13; J. Daniel Rogers, "Patterns of Change on the Western Margin of the Southeast, A.D. 600–900," in *Stability, Transformation, and Variation: The Late Woodlands Southeast*, ed. Michael S. Nassaney and Charles R. Cobb (New York: Plenum Press, 1991), pp. 221–33; Newcomb, *Indians of Texas*, pp. 16–18; William T. Field, *The Indians of Texas* (San Antonio: Institute of Texan Cultures, 1982), pp. 3–5.

5. For a summary of the political, social, and economic lives of the East Texas Caddos including the Tejas, see James M. Smallwood, *Born in Dixie: The History of Smith County, Texas*, vol. 2 (Austin: Eakin Press, 1999), pp. 4–25; also see Worthington, *Prehistoric Indians of the Southwest*, pp. 20–23. For detail, see Vynol Beaver Newkumet, *Hasinai: A Traditional History of the Caddo Confederacy* (College Station: Texas A&M University Press, 1988) and Perttula's *Caddo Nation*. An older work is George A. Dorsey, *Traditions of the Caddo* (Washington, D.C.: Carnegie Institution, 1905). Also see

Herbert E. Bolton, *The Hasinai: South Caddoans as Seen by the Earliest Europeans* (reprint, Norman: University of Oklahoma Press, 1987).

6. For more detail, see Lawrence E. Aten, *Indians of the Upper Texas Coast* (New York: Academic Press, 1983); Andre Sjoberg, "The Bidai Indians of Southeastern Texas" (master's thesis, University of Texas, 1951); and Mildred P. Mayhall, "The Indians of Texas: The Atakapa, the Karankawa, the Tonkawa" (Ph.D. diss., University of Texas, 1939). For a short summary, see Newcomb, *Indians of Texas,* pp. 315–29.

7. Robert S. Weddle, *Wilderness Manhunt: The Spanish Search for La Salle* (Austin: University of Texas Press, 1973), pp. 139–48.

8. A good source of information about the Karankawas and the Coahuiltecans is Álvar Núñez Cabeza de Vaca, "The Narrative of Álvar Núñez Cabeza de Vaca," in *Spanish Explorers of the Southern United States, 1528–1543,* ed. Frederick Webb Hodge (New York: n.p., 1907), pp. 12–128; also Newcomb, *Indians of Texas,* pp. 29–81; Albert S. Gatschet, *The Karankawa Indians, the Coast People of Texas* (Cambridge, Mass.: Peabody Museum of American Archaeology and Ethnology, 1891) and Robert A. Ricklis, *The Karankawa Indians of Texas: An Ecological Study of Cultural Tradition and Change* (Austin: University of Texas Press, 1996).

9. David La Vere, *A History of the Indians of Texas,* (College Station: Texas A&M University Press, 2004).

10. In his narrative, Cabeza de Vaca offers observations about the Jumano. For detail, see Parrott Hickerson, *Jumano: Hunters and Traders of the South Plains* (Austin: University of Texas Press, 1994); for brief coverage, see Newcomb, *Indians of Texas,* pp. 225–45.

11. For information on the Plains tribes, see Newcomb, *Indians of Texas,* pp. 85–221; also see Betty Gerald, *Comanche Society: Before the Reservation* (College Station: Texas A&M University Press, 2002); Earnest Wallace and E. Adamson Hoebel, *The Comanches* (Norman: University of Oklahoma Press, 1952); Howard L. Meredith, *Dancing on Common Ground: Tribal Cultures and Alliances on the Southern Plains* (Lawrence: University Press of Kansas, 1995); Mildred P. Mayhall, *The Kiowas,* 2d ed. (Norman: University of Oklahoma Press, 1962); Thomas Schilz, *Lipan Apaches in Texas* (El Paso: Texas Western Press, 1987); and Paul H. Carlson, *The Plains Indians* (College Station: Texas A&M University Press, 1998).

12. Robert Onco in La Vere, *Life among the Texas Indians,* p. 125.

CHAPTER 2. INVASIONS OF THE EUROPEANS AND AMERICANS

1. The best source for information on Cabeza de Vaca is his journal: De Vaca, "The Narrative of Álvar Núñez Cabeza de Vaca" in *Spanish Explorers,* ed. Hodge; effects of diseases are mentioned in La Vere, *Life among the Texas Indians,* pp. 10–11; and for more details see John C. Ewers, "The Influence of Epidemics on other Indian Populations and Cultures of Texas," *Plains Anthropologist* 18 (May, 1973): 104–55.

▼▼▼

2. La Vere, *History of the Indians of Texas;* see Ewers, "The Influence of Epidemics," pp. 104–15.

3. Information about De Soto's expedition can be found in Lawrence A. Clayton, ed., *The De Soto Chronicles: The Expedition of Hernando de Soto to North American 1539–1543,* vol. 2 (Tuscaloosa: University of Alabama Press, 1993).

4. La Vere, *Life among the Texas Indians,* pp. 11–14; Newcomb, *Indians of Texas,* pp. 85–101. For more details on the impact of the horse on Indian cultures, see Preston Holder, *The Hoe and the Horse on the Plains: A Study of Cultural Development among North American Indians* (Lincoln: University of Nebraska Press, 1970).

5. For more on the European invasions of Texas, see Elizabeth A. H. John, *Storms Brewed in Other Men's Worlds: The Confrontation of Indians, Spanish, and French in the Southwest, 1540–1795* (Lincoln: University of Nebraska Press, 1981) and Henry Folmer, *Franco-Spanish Rivalry in North America, 1524–1763* (Glendale: A. H. Clark, 1953). Also see the older work by William E. Dunn, *Spanish and French Rivalry in the Gulf Region of the United States, 1678–1702* (Austin: Texas State Historical Association, 1948).

6. For information on La Salle's doomed expedition see *The Journal of Henri Joutel, 1684–1687,* ed. William C. Foster, trans. Johanna S. Warren (Austin: Texas State Historical Association, 1998), pp. 226–77.

7. The best sources for accurate information about the Lady in Blue are T. D. Kendrick, *Mary of Ágreda: The Life and Legend of a Spanish Nun* (London: Routledge & Kegan Paul Ltd., 1967) and William H. Donahue, "Mary of Ágreda and the Southwest United States," *The Americas* 9, no. 3 (1953): 291–314.

8. La Vere, *History of the Indians of Texas.*

9. Information on the Tonkawas can be found in Newcomb, *Indians of Texas,* pp. 22, 134–41; La Vere, *Life among the Texas Indians,* 8–9; and R. E. Moore, "The Tonkawa Indians," Internet: www.TexasIndians.com/ton.

10. Quote is from R. Edward Moore, "The Tigua Indians of Texas," Internet: www.TexasIndians.com. For additional information on Tiguas see Bill Wright, *The Tiguas: Pueblo Indians of Texas* (El Paso: Texas Western Press, 1993) and Joe S. Sando, *The Pueblo Indians* (San Francisco: Indians Historian Press, 1976).

11. For more information on the Apaches, see Tomas E. Mails, *The People Called Apache* (Englewood Cliffs: Prentice-Hall, 1974); Schilz, *Lipan Apaches in Texas;* and John Upton Terrell, *The Plains Apache* (New York: Crowell, 1975).

12. Tom Guderjan and Carol Canty, *The Indian Texans* (reprint, San Antonio: Institute of Texan Cultures, 1994), p. 17.

13. Mihecaby quote in La Vere, *Life among the Texas Indians,* p. 78. For information on the Comanche, see Wallace and Hoebel, *The Comanches;* Gerald, *Comanche Society;* and Carlson, *The Plains Indians.*

14. La Vere, *Life among the Texas Indians,* p. 95.

15. Ibid., p. 78.

16. Quote by Mrs. John Barnes in ibid., pp. 90–91.

17. Rachel Plummer, *Rachael Plummer's Narrative of Twenty-One Months Ser-*

▼▼▼

vitude as a Prisoner among the Commanchee Indians (Austin: Jenkins Publishing Company, 1977), p. 14.

18. Coronado quote in Rebecca Brush, "The Wichita Indians," Internet: www.TexasIndians.com/Wichita.

19. Ibid., pp. 1–11. For more detail, see Robert Bell, Edward B. Jelks, and W. W. Newcomb, *Wichita Indians* (New York: Garland, 1974); F. Todd Smith, *The Wichita Indians: Traders of Texas and the Southern Plains, 1540–1845* (College Station: Texas A&M University Press, 1976); and Earl H. Elam, "The History of the Wichita Confederation to 1868" (Ph.D. diss., Texas Tech University, 1971).

20. Lesley Byrd Simpson, ed., Paul D. Nathan, trans., *The San Sabá Papers: A Documentary Account of the Founding and Destruction of San Sabá Mission* (Dallas: Southern Methodist University Press, 2000); Robert S. Weddle, *San Sabá Mission: Spanish Pivot in Texas* (College Station: Texas A&M University Press, 1999).

21. For early American involvement in Texas, see Harris G. Warren, *The Sword Was Their Passport: A History of American Filibustering in the Mexican Revolution* (Baton Rouge: Louisiana State University); also see Maurine T. Wilson and Jack Jackson, *Philip Nolan and Texas: Expeditions into the Unknown Land, 1791–1801* (Waco: Texian Press, 1987).

22. For a survey of immigrant Indians and their relationship with the Texas revolutionaries and the later Republic of Texas, see Smallwood, *Born in Dixie,* 1:25–59.

23. For additional information on gift giving, see La Vere, *Life among the Texas Indians,* pp. 35–36, 113, 120–22, 171–72.

24. For more information on the Council House fight and Comanche-Anglo relations, see Walter Prescott Webb, *The Texas Rangers* (reprint, Austin: University of Texas Press, 1982); Noah Smithwick, *The Evolution of a State, or Recollections of Old Texas Days* (reprint, Austin: University of Texas Press, 1983); Wallace and Hoebel, *The Comanches;* and Thomas W. Kavanagh, *Comanche Political History: An Ethnohistorical Perspective, 1706–1875* (Lincoln: University of Nebraska Press, 1995).

25. For information about additional Indian raids and captive-taking, see J. W. Wilbarger, *Indian Depredations in Texas* (reprint, Austin: Eakin Press, 1985); for details on the Council House fight and its consequences see Donaly E. Brice, *The Great Comanche Raid of 1840* (Austin: Eakin Press, 1987).

26. For information about the failure of the reservation policy and the broader story of Indians in western Texas see Kenneth F. Neighbors, *Robert Simpson Neighbors and the Texas Frontier* (Waco: Texian Press, 1975); also consult the older work of Virginia Pink Noel, "The United States Indian Reservations in Texas, 1854–1859" (master's thesis, University of Texas, 1924).

27. See George Henry Pettis, *Kit Carson's Fight with the Comanche and Kiowa Indians at the Adobe Walls* (reprint, Santa Fe: n.p., 1908) for information on the Battle at Adobe Walls. For more about Kit Carson's career, see M. Morgan Estergreen, *Kit Carson: A Portrait in Courage* (Norman: University of Oklahoma Press, 1963). For the treaties and the larger story of the defeat of the southern Plains Indians, see

William Leckie, *Military Conquest of the Southern Plains* (Norman: University of Oklahoma Press, 1963). For a brief account of the treaty process, see William T. Hagan, *United States–Comanche Relations: The Reservation Years*, 2d ed. (Norman: University of Oklahoma Press, 1990), pp. 44–48.

28. Stanley Noyes, *Comanches in the New West, 1895–1908* (Austin: University of Texas Press, 1999), p. 3.

CHAPTER 3. THE CONTINUING STRUGGLE TO SURVIVE

1. For information on the last of the Indian campaigns, see Carlson, *The Plains Indians;* John Edward Weems, *Death Song: The Last of the Indian Wars* (Garden City: Doubleday, 1976); James L. Hailey, *The Buffalo War: The History of the Red River Uprising of 1874* (Garden City: Doubleday, 1976); and Robert Utley, *Frontier Regulars: The United States Army and the Indians, 1866–1891* (New York: Macmillan, 1973).

2. Kevin Mulroy, *Freedom on the Border: The Seminole Maroons in Florida, the Indian Territory, Coahuila, and Texas* (Lubbock: Texas Tech Press, 1993).

3. Information about the extermination of the buffalo can be found in William Temple Hornaday, *The Extermination of the American Bison* (Washington, D.C.: Government Printing Office, 1889) and John R. Cook, *The Border and the Buffalo: An Untold Story of the Southwest Plains* (reprint, New York: Citadel Press, 1967). To learn more about the First Battle of Adobe Walls, see Pettis, *Kit Carson's Fight.*

4. La Vere, *Life among the Texas Indians*, pp. 70–71.

5. For Ranald Mackenzie and the Red River War, see Earnest Wallace, *Ranald S. Mackenzie on the Texas Frontier* (Lubbock: West Texas Museum Association, 1964) and Robert G. Carter, *On the Border with Mackenzie, or Winning the West from the Comanches* (Washington: Eynon Press, 1935). For more on Parker, see Clyde L. Jackson and Grace Jackson, *Quanah Parker* (New York: Exposition Press, 1963).

6. See Joseph A. Stout, Jr., *Apache Lighting: The Last Great Battles of the Oho Calientes* (New York: Oxford University Press, 1974); William H. Leckie, *The Buffalo Soldiers* (Norman: University of Oklahoma Press, 1967); and James Kaywaykla, *In the Days of Victorio* (Tucson: University of Arizona Press, 1970).

7. See Robert A. Wooster, *The Military and United States Indian Policy, 1865–1903* (New Haven: Yale University Press, 1988) for reformers and policy.

CHAPTER 4. FROM SURVIVAL TO REVIVAL

1. Population figures can be obtained in U.S. Bureau of the Census documents.

2. See the videotape *Big City Trail: The Urban Indians of Texas* (San Antonio: Institute of Texan Cultures, 1994) and the teacher's guide by Barbara Evans Stanush; *Dallas Morning News*, Sept. 1, 1989.

▼▼▼

3. For more on the Alabama-Coushatta tribe, see www.alabama-coushatta.com/history; modern-era information is in *Dallas Morning News,* May 4, 2001; *Los Angeles Times,* Oct. 8, 2000; and *Houston Chronicle,* Apr. 23, 2000. Also see Texas Indian Commission, *The Texas Indian Commission on the American Indians in Texas* (Austin: Texas Indian Commission, 1986). One of the better sources about the tribe is the videotape *Circle of Life: The Alabama-Coushattas* (San Antonio: Institute of Texan Cultures, 1992) and the teacher's guide by Barbara Evans Stanush. The controversy over the tribe's casino is addressed in *Houston Chronicle,* Apr. 29, 2001, and *Fort Worth Star-Telegram,* May 8, 2001.

4. For more on the Tigua tribe, see the videotape *People of the Sun: The Tiguas of Ysleta* (San Antonio: Institute of Texan Cultures, 1994) and the teacher's guide by Barbara Evan Stanush. For glimpses of the tribe in the modern era, also see *Dallas Morning News,* July 31, 2000, and for the controversy over the Tiguas' casino, see *Fort Worth Star-Telegram,* May 8, 2001.

5. For information on the Kickapoos in the modern era see *San Diego Union-Tribune,* Nov. 22, 1985; *Los Angles Times,* Apr. 8, 1985; and *San Francisco Chronicle,* Nov. 22, 1985. For further information about their casino, see *Fort Worth Star-Telegram,* May 8, 2001, and *Dallas Morning News,* Aug. 23, 1997.

6. For information on textbooks, see Mark Yudof, "Multicultural History: Texas Textbooks Keep Good Perspective," *Dallas Morning News,* Sept. 1, 2001; for more on protests over state monuments, see Clay Robison, "Lots of Room for New Statues: Bill Seeks Greater Ethnic Diversity in State Monuments," *Houston Chronicle,* Mar. 2, 2001.

7. Cultural differences and misunderstandings are addressed in *Dallas Morning News,* Sept. 26, 1992.

8. Angela K. Brown, "Indian Mascots Causing Controversy for some Texas Schools," *Associated Press Newswires,* Sept. 5, 2001.

▼▼▼

Selected Bibliography

Carlson, Paul H. *The Plains Indians.* College Station: Texas A&M University Press, *1998.*

John, Elizabeth A. H. *Storms Brewed in Other Men's Worlds: The Confrontation of Indians, Spanish, and French in the Southwest, 1540-1795.* Lincoln: University of Nebraska Press, *1981.*

La Vere, David. *Life among the Texas Indians: The WPA Narratives.* College Station: Texas A&M University Press, *1998.*

La Vere, David. *A History of the Indians of Texas.* College Station: Texas A&M University Press, *2004.*

Leckie, William. *Military Conquest of the Southern Plains.* Norman: University of Oklahoma Press, *1963.*

Meredith, Howard. *Dancing on Common Ground: Tribal Cultures and Alliances on the Southern Plains.* Lawrence: University Press of Kansas, *1996.*

Newcomb, W. W. *The Indians of Texas from Prehistory to Modern Times.* Austin: University of Texas Press, *1961.*

Texas Indian Commission. *The Texas Indian Commission and American Indians in Texas.* Austin: Texas Indian Commission, *1986.*

Utley, Robert M. *Frontier Regulars: the United States Army and the Indians, 1866-1891.* New York: Macmillan, *1973.*

Wright, Bill. *The Tiguas: Pueblo Indians of Texas.* El Paso: Texas Western Press, *1993.*

VIDEOTAPES

Big City Trail: the Urban Indians of Texas (with teacher's guide). San Antonio: Institute of Texan Cultures. *1992.*

Circle of Life: The Alabama-Coushattas (with teacher's guide). San Antonio: Institute of Texan Cultures, *1992.*

People of the Sun: The Tiguas of Ysleta (with teacher's guide). San Antonio: Institute of Texan Cultures, *1994.*

Index

▼▼▼

▼▼▼

ISBN 1-58544-354-9

90000